CW01510529

Complete Rosicrucian Initiations of the Fellowship of the Rosy Cross

Arthur E. Waite

Ishtar Publishing
www.ishtarpublishing.com

ISBN (13) 978-0-9783883-4-8 (Hb.)

Book Design: Mamdouh Al-Daye
Cover Designer and Artwork: Athena Amato

Ishtar Publishing
141-6200 McKay Avenue,
Suite 716,
Burnaby, BC
Canada V5H-4M9
www.ishtarpublishing.com

TABLE OF CONTENTS

Issued by Frater Sacramentum Regis
Most Honoured Imperator
In Ordine Rosea Crucis
For the Direction of Celebrants and
The Use of Fratres et Sorores Under the
Obedience of Authorized Temples

The First Order Of The Rosy Cross

World of Action
Part III

Solemn Festival of the Equinox

As it is essential to the symbolism of this ceremonial observance that it should take place concurrently with the event that it exists to commemorate in ritual, deviation from the due-date is permitted only in cases of recognized necessity, as e.g., when the Equinox falls on a Sunday and from the external circumstances of the place of meeting or those of the members at large, it may be difficult or indeed impossible to hold a celebration on that day. The average due dates are reckoned as March 21 and September 21.

If any grades of the Fellowship are conferred at the same convocation, the Festival of the Equinox shall be celebrated last of all.

The officers required for the observance are the Imperator of the Fellowship or, him failing, his substitute appointed previously, and those of the Neophyte Grade.

The arrangement of the temple is shown in the official diagram of that grade, and the temple is opened therein, unless this has been done previously for the admission of a Novice.

MASTER OF THE TEMPLE: Fratres et Sorores of the holy and glorious Order of the Rosy Cross, in virtue of the power to me committed, and with the grace of your devout assistance, we will proceed to commemorate the occurrence of the Vernal (*vel Autumnal*) Equinox (*knocks once*).

All rise. The Master of the Temple lifts up his arms holding his wand of office, and says with raised face and eyes;

MASTER OF THE TEMPLE: To the glory of God in the highest, and to the brightness of the Everlasting Light.

The pause of a moment follows.

MASTER OF THE TEMPLE: Auxiliary Frater Zelator, lift up the lamp of your office: a light shall shine upon our ways.

The Auxiliary Frater Zelator passes directly to the western side of the altar and, facing east, he lifts up his lamp and wand.

MASTER OF THE TEMPLE: The Light of the Lord shall lead us. You have my command to declare the Equinox. He shall ordain a lamp for His anointed.

FRATER ZELATOR: Blessed be the Name of the Lord, in the Temple which is called by His Name and the Place of His Sanctuary. By the Holy and Incommunicable Word, and under the ordinance of our Honourable Master, I declare the Vernal *(vel Autumnal)* Equinox.

The Auxiliary Frater Zelator returns direct to his place.

MASTER OF THE TEMPLE: (*Knocks once*) He shall quench not the lamp of Israel.

The Imperator rises from his seat, which is between the thrones of the Celebrants in the due east, but at a little distance behind them. He goes forward in advance of the thrones.

3

IMPERATOR: The Lord preserve our inheritance. By the power in me vested as Keeper of the Sacred Mystery, I proclaim the revocation of the temporal password * * * * *

The Imperator returns to his seat.

MASTER OF THE TEMPLE: Thy Word is the fountain of wisdom. The Word shall preserve Thy children and the part of Thine inheritance forever. Confirm Thou Thy Word upon us.

This is said with raised eyes and uplifted wand. The pause of a moment follows.

MASTER OF THE TEMPLE: Let us sanctify with due worship the mystic festival of the Equinox. Seal us at Thy feasts, O Lord, in the house of Thy foundation, the place of praise for Thy people. We have set our house in order; the altar and house are sanctified.

The Master of the Temple gives a battery of one knock.

MASTER OF THE TEMPLE: Light of the world without. Shadow of the world within.

FRATER ZELATOR: Darkness of material things. Obscure night of the soul.

MASTER OF THE TEMPLE: Orient of the cosmic world. Golden dawn of the spirit. Life and the Life of life. Gate of entrance.

FRATER ZELATOR: Land of the setting sun. Passing of the soul in glory. Gate of going forth.

GUIDE OF THE PATHS: Clear height of the air. Stellar spaces. Mind which the Lord hath moved. Show unto us Thy Mind, O Lord.

WARDEN OF THE TEMPLE: Waters of the world without. Water of Life. The soul is a great sea. Pass over the waters of the soul. Come to us in the great waters.

The Guide of the Paths gives a battery of one knock. He extends his arms.

GUIDE OF THE PATHS: Peace of reconciliation. Peace between the east and west. Equipoise and harmony of all. Marriage of heaven and earth. I am the reconciler between them.

The Imperator rises from his seat and goes forward in advance of the thrones. The Auxiliary Frater Zelator passes directly to the western side of the altar and facing east, he lifts up his lamp and wand.

FRATER ZELATOR: Silence in the Mouth of the Almighty One.

The Imperator gives the sign of a Neophyte.

IMPERATOR: Fratres et Sorores, in the union of body and mind, and with the mystical sign of the grade, seek for the reconciliation that is within. In the silence of the lips, my brethren.

All present repeat the sign. The Imperator and Auxiliary Frater Zelator return directly to their places. The Master of the Temple gives a battery of one knock.

FRATER THURIFICANS: Summer's heat and harvest. Fervent zeal of desire, kindled in the sons of the doctrine.

He lifts up his smoking thurible and offers incense in the west.

FRATER AQUARIUS: Winter's frost and cold. Restoring sleep of nature. Sleep of the Divine in man. Life-giving rain of doctrine.

He lifts up his vessel of water and sprinkles Water in the west.

FRATER THURIFICANS: House of the sun in its zenith. Realm of clemency. Turn our captivity, O Lord, as a stream in the South.

He offers incense as before.

FRATER AQUARIUS: Gate of the north. Holiness is in the gate of Thy judgment. Show unto us Thy sun of justice.

He sprinkles water as before.

MASTER OF THE TEMPLE: Fire of the world without. Holy Fire of the will. Fire of Divine Law. Baptise us with Holy Fire.

FRATER ZELATOR: Earth, which is the footstool of spirit. Body, which the spirit cleanses. Purify our earthly part.

The Guide of the Paths gives a battery of one knock. He extends his arms.

GUIDE OF THE PATHS: Peace between the north and the south. Peace between the times and seasons. Peace of the earthly part. Peace of the will in union. I am the reconciler between them.

The Imperator rises from his seat and goes forward in advance of the thrones. The Auxiliary Frater Zelator passes directly to the western side of the altar and facing east, he lifts up his lamp and wand.

FRATER ZELATOR: Silence in the Mouth of the Almighty One.

The Imperator gives the sign of a Neophyte.

IMPERATOR: Fratres et Sorores, in the union of heart and will, and with the mystical sign of the grade, seek for the peace that is within. In the silence of the heart, my brethren.

All present repeat the sign. The Imperator and Auxiliary Frater Zelator return directly to their places. The Master of the Temple gives a battery of one knock.

WARDEN OF THE TEMPLE: Soul suspiring.

MASTER OF THE TEMPLE: Will sustaining.

GUIDE OF THE PATHS: Mind concurring.

FRATER ZELATOR: Body, as the vehicle of all.

The Guide of the Paths gives a battery of one knock. He extends his arms.

GUIDE OF THE PATHS: Quintessence, Summum Bonum, self-knowing Spirit.   I am the reconciler in all things.

The Imperator rises from his seat and goes forward in advance of the thrones. The Auxiliary Frater Zelator passes direct to the western side of the altar and, facing east, he lifts up his lamp and wand.

FRATER ZELATOR: Silence in the Mouth of the Almighty One.

The Imperator gives the sign of a Neophyte.

IMPERATOR: Fratres et Sorores, in the union of the soul and its purpose, and with the mystical sign of the grade, seek for the Spirit that is within. In the silence of the soul, my brethren.

All present repeat the Sign. The Imperator and Auxiliary Frater Zelator return directly to their places. The unofficial members are seated. The Master of the Temple descends from his throne, passes directly through the pillars and thence proceeds by south to the western side of the altar. He elevates his wand, with his face upraised.

MASTER OF THE TEMPLE: In the Name of God, Who is my strength, I received the wand of my office. At the revocation of the password *****, I lay it down in peace. (*He crosses himself.*) In peace, in that I will sleep and will rest in the mercy of Thy service, my Lord and my God. (*He has laid his wand against the altar and has taken up the lamp of fire. He holds it with both hands in front of him.*) Plead with us, O Lord, in our flesh; purge us with Thy refining fire.

He returns by north to the pillars, thence directly to his throne, where he stands in front of the pedestal, facing west and holding the lamp in his hands. The Warden of the Temple descends from his throne, passes directly through the pillars and thence proceeds by the south to the western side of the altar. With face upraised, he elevates his wand.

9

WARDEN OF THE TEMPLE: In the Name of the Lord of Hosts, I received the wand of my office. At the revocation of the password *****, I lay it down in purity. (*He crosses himself.*) Thy counsel is a Tree of Life. Deliver me by the strength of Thine hands, that I may keep the mystery of faith with a clean heart. (*He has laid his wand against the altar and has taken the cup of sacramental wine. He holds it with both hands in front of him.*) Thine are the vials of gold, and the golden cups are Thine. The Lord is the portion of my chalice; my cup runneth over.

He returns by north to the pillars, thence directly to his throne, where he stands in front of the pedestal, facing west and holding the cup in his hands.

The chair of the Guide has been set aside. He passes from the middle place of the pillars to the western side of the altar, following the sun. With face upraised, he elevates his wand.

GUIDE OF THE PATHS: In the Name of Messias the Prince, I received the wand of my office for the work of redemption, O Lord, in the temple of Thy service. At the revocation of the password *****, I lay it down in perfect charity. (*He crosses himself.*) My scepter, O Lord, shall not depart from this temple till the coming of the Peace-Maker. (*He has laid his wand against the altar and taken the Sacramental Rose. He holds it with both hands in front of him.*) The mind which looks to Thee is a Rose that unfolds in Thy Light.

He passes round the altar by the north and turns at the eastern side, facing west. The Auxiliary Frater Zelator goes up directly from his place to the west of the altar. With face upraised, he elevates his lamp and wand.

FRATER ZELATOR: In the Name of the holy and beautiful Light, Light of the mind and heart, Light of the desiring soul and the Holy Spirit in man, I received my lamp and wand. At the revocation of the password *****, I lay down my wand of office. Do you, O Honourable Guide, receive this sacred lamp and guard the fire thereof in the mystery that we are about to perform.

He crosses himself.

GUIDE OF THE PATHS: This Rose also shall pass through to you, and you shall receive it from my hands, a sign of the bond of union between the worlds above and below.

They have passed from one to another the Sacramental Rose and the mystic lamp, saying:

GUIDE OF THE PATHS: In the light of understanding the Lord shall lead His people.

FRATER ZELATOR *(extending the Rose before him with both hands)*: The Rose of Thy benediction, O Lord, is a pure essence of Life.

The Frater Zelator has laid down his wand against the altar and passes with the Rose to a middle place between the altar and the west, where he faces east.

The Guide of the Paths returns to the pillars, stands between them and there lifts up the lamp.

GUIDE OF THE PATHS: The uncorrupted splendor of the law is the brightness of Everlasting Light. O kindle Thy justice as a star.

He lowers the lamp. The Frater Thurificans goes direct from his place to the western side of the altar and there raises his vessel of Fire, saying with uplifted face:

FRATER THURIFICANS: In the Name of our fire of longing, I received the thurible of my office. At the revocation of the password *******, I lay down the hallowing vessel. (*He crosses himself.*) O Lord, our souls shall burn as a perpetual incense before Thee. (*He has laid his thurible on the altar and has taken up the paten of bread, holding it in his two hands.*) Satisfy us with the bread of Heaven, O Lord. Visit us in the giving of bread.

The Frater Thurificans goes directly to his proper place in the west, where he remains standing, holding the paten.

The Frater Aquarius moves directly from his place to the western side of the altar and there raises his vessel of water, saying with uplifted face:

FRATER AQUARIUS: In the name of the water of salvation, flowing from the temple which is above, I received the vessel of my office. At the revocation of the password ******, I lay down the purifying symbol. (*He crosses himself.*) I have seen that Water flowing; the soul is whiter than snow which is washed thereby. (*He has laid his vessel on the altar and has taken up the platter of salt, holding it in his two hands.*) Savor me with the salt of wisdom, O Lord. Remember the salt of Thy covenant.

The Frater Aquarius goes directly to his proper station, where he takes up his place and stands holding the platter.

The Imperator gives a battery of one knock. All rise. With wand lifted up and alone, the Imperator of the Rite begins his solemn circumambulation of the temple, proceeding from his place in the east. When he readies the middle south he turns directly thereto. Celebrants and members face the same quarter. The Master of the Temple uplifts his lamp.

IMPERATOR: I saw, as it were, a sea of glass, mingled with fire. In the Name of Thy Holy Shekinah and by the White Rose of Thy mercy, come to us in the baptism of the Spirit, O Lord. Kindle us with Thy saving fire. Be the fire of Thy zeal in Zion, that we may do the will of our Father.

The Imperator of the Rite makes the sign of the Cosmic Cross with his wand. The Imperator passes to the west, while is faced by all present. The Fratres Thurificans et Aquarius lift up the bread and salt.

IMPERATOR: The kingdom of earth is Thine, and the kingdom to which we are called. In the Name of Thy Holy Shekinah and by the union of red and white in the Mystical Rose of benignity, awaken us to the life that is eternal. May Thy kingdom be declared in us. May it reign in our earthly part, as in the Spirit which is Thine, from henceforth and forever. So shalt Thou give us from day to day our super-substantial bread.

The Imperator of the Rite makes the sign of the Cosmic Cross with his wand and passes thereafter to the middle north, which is faced by all present. The Warden of the Temple raises his sacramental cup.

IMPERATOR: The Spirit of God moved upon the waters of Creation, and the life of the universe began. Spirit of the Life of life, move upon the waters of the soul. In the Name of Thy Holy Shekinah and by the Red Rose of Thy justice, show unto us the ineffable mysteries which abide therein. Show unto us Thy Sacred Presence abiding in the soul of man.

The Imperator of the Rite makes the sign of the Cosmic Cross with his wand. He passes thereafter to the mideast, between the thrones of the Celebrants, but a little in front of them. All face east. The Auxiliary Frater Zelator lifts up the Rose.

IMPERATOR: Thou didst call the firmament Heaven. We praise Thee in the firmament of Thy power. In the Name of Thy Holy Shekinah, by the union of Jehovah and Elohim, show unto us Thy mind, O Lord. Give us the desire thereof.

The Imperator of the Rite makes the sign of the Cosmic Cross with his wand. The Imperator returns to his seat and stands thereby. All face as usual.

The Guide of the Paths lifts up the lamp of the Lucifer, standing between the pillars.

GUIDE OF THE PATHS: My spirit has descended into the deep, O Lord, and has found Thee in the dark regions. My spirit has gone up into the heights and has adored Thee in places of concealment, before the Throne of Thy Glory. At the extremities of the universe and the end of all the spaces, I have known Thy Holy Presence. I have found Thee in the palace at the Center. I am the self-knowing spirit — O God, my God — and I have realized Thee in my inmost being. O Lord, Thy Light is our service; the Light is Thine aid extended. Give unto us the equal light, Thou sun of our souls. Give unto us the quintessential light, to complete our human nature. Thou Who has made us in Thine image, remember us by that glorious likeness. Deliver us from the obscure night. Shine on us from the zenith of Thy knowledge; show unto us the vision which is Thou. Let us live in Thy pure Light, Thy full Light, in Thy high Light forever.

He makes the sign of the Cosmic Cross with the lamp of the Lucifer. The Imperator speaks from his place.

IMPERATOR: O honorable Master of the Temple, the end of this time is upon us, and that which remains to be done thou shalt do quickly.

What follows takes place in complete silence. The unofficial members are seated. The Master of the Temple passes to the western side of the altar, lifts up and lays down his Lamp, returns with the sun to his throne, deposits his robe and collar thereon, and takes a seat proper to his grade among the unofficial members. The same form is observed by the other officers in succession, the Guide of the Paths coming last. He raises the lamp of the Lucifer to its full height and passes in this manner to the altar. As he stands at the western end, facing east, the lamp being still lifted up, he says:

GUIDE OF THE PATHS: Selah.

He puts down the lamp. All the officers have deposited their robes and collars on their respective seats and have found their proper places in the body general of the temple. All present being seated, there follows a short pause. The Imperator rises and goes before the thrones in the east.

IMPERATOR: The mystery of the Equinox is perfect in all degrees. I declare the offices of the temple suspended. The rite is in the hands of the headship, and the headship is under the providence of God.

He returns to his seat; another pause follows, and thereafter he again rises, but remains in his place.

IMPERATOR: There Was Silence In Heaven For The Space of Half-An-Hour.

The Frater Ostiarius rises in his place.

FRATER OSTIARIUS: Brethren of the First and Second Orders, arise and follow me.

He opens the door and, with wand uplifted, leads them forth from the temple.

The ceremony of installing the new Master is performed in accordance with the authorized ritual. At its conclusion one of the brethren of the Third Order passes to the door, which he throws open and says:

FRATER ADEPTUS MINOR: The brethren of the First and Second Orders will resume their places in the temple.

They are led in by the Frater Ostiarius, with wand lifted up, and when all are seated, the Imperator rises and goes before the thrones in the east.

IMPERATOR: By virtue of the power in me vested, I proclaim the Restoration of the Rite, and I communicate to you the secret word *****, to prevail as a temporal password during the ensuing six months. May the grace of its sacrament be poured abundantly upon all. (*A pause.*) By virtue of the power in me vested, I announce that the solemn ceremonies of this temple will be discharged as set forth herein.

He reads the list of official appointments and then continues as follows;

IMPERATOR: Fratres et Sorores of the Fellowship of the Rosy Cross, behold your Master, the honorable Frater Signum Lucis (*vel nomen aliud*), who has been regularly installed and enthroned. By the power in me vested, I proclaim him the revealer of mysteries among you for the six months intervening between the Vernal and Autumnal Equinox (*vel vice versa*), being part of that temporal period through which we are led into the light. Honorable Frater Signum Lucis (*vel nomen aliud*), in the presence of the sons and daughters of your temple, I call upon you to make your confession.

He resumes his seat. The Master of the Temple rises and recites the ensuing:

CONFESSION

Fratres et Sorores of the Order: Seeing that the whole intention of the lesser mysteries, or of external initiation, is so to lead the soul — by the intervention of symbol, ceremonial and sacrament — that it may be withdrawn from the attraction of matter and delivered from the absorption therein, whereby it walks in somnambulism, knowing not whence it cometh nor whither it goeth: Seeing also that, thus withdrawn, the soul must be brought, under true direction, to the study of Divine things, that it may offer the only clean oblation and acceptable sacrifice, which is Love reaching outward and inward to God, man and the universe: Now therefore, I confess and testify hereunto from my throne in this temple;

and I promise, so far as in me lies, to lead you by the rites of the Fellowship, faithfully conserved and exhibited with becoming reverence, that through such love and such sacrifice you may be prepared in due time for the greater mysteries, the supreme and interior initiation.

In the absence of a special representation on the part of the new Master, this confession shall be read from the vellum scroll on which it is inscribed.

The Master of the Temple resumes his seat. The investiture of officers follows and should be performed by the Master of the Temple, since the right inheres in his office, as well as in that of the Imperator, who, for purposes of convenience, usually assists in the clothing.

Master of the Temple (knocks once): By virtue of the power to me committed, I proceed to invest my officers.

He cites each in succession by name, and each is brought to his pedestal by the Imperator, or him failing, the Immediate Past Master, who bears the clothing and insignia particular to each office, the wands and instruments included. The newly-appointed Warden of the Temple is brought first to the east, and being invested with cloak and collar:

MASTER OF THE TEMPLE: By the power to me committed, I ordain you Warden of this Temple until the next festival of the Equinox. I pray that from your throne in the east you may lead the Fratres et Sorores to the full light of the end. I present you with your wand of office. May it symbolize to you and to the brethren that God is known of the heart.

WARDEN OF THE TEMPLE: In the Name of the Lord of Hosts, and by the word ******, I receive my wand of office and accept the duties which it signifies as a servant of God and my brethren in the sacred bonds of the Order.

He passes directly to his throne in the north-east and takes his seat thereon. The newly-appointed Guide of the Paths is led to the east and invested in the same manner.

MASTER OF THE TEMPLE: By the power to me committed, I ordain you Guide of the Paths and Grades until the next festival of the Equinox, and I pray that — between the pillars — you may lead the Fratres et Sorores into the equilibrium of perfect reconciliation. I present you with your wand of office. May it symbolize to you and to the brethren that God is seen of the mind, when the eye of mind is open unto Divine Light.

GUIDE OF THE PATHS: In the Name of Messias the Prince, and by the word ******, I receive my wand of office and accept the duties which it signifies as a servant of God and my brethren.

The Guide of the Paths passes with the sun to his place between the pillars and takes his seat.

The newly-appointed Auxiliary Frater Zelator is led to the east and invested.

MASTER OF THE TEMPLE: By the power to me committed, I ordain you Proclamator and Lucifer of this temple until the next festival of the Equinox. It is your part to go before the Postulants with the torch of the higher luminaries, uttering the watchwords of the day. Thanks be to God, my brother, for the admirable light which illuminates our earthly part. I present you with your wand of office. May it symbolize to you and to the brethren that perfect purification of our humanity which is attained in the life of the Cross. Receive also this lamp, and see that your light is burning.

FRATER ZELATOR: In the Name of the Secret Light, and by the Word ******, I receive my wand and lamp, accepting the duties which they signify as a servant of God and my brethren.

The Auxiliary Frater Zelator passes with the sun to his place in the due west and takes his seat.

The newly-appointed Frater Thurificans is led to the east and invested.

MASTER OF THE TEMPLE: By the power to me committed, I ordain you Thurificans of this temple until the next festival of the Equinox, to watch over the fires of the temple and to perform the consecrations by fire. Remember the sweet odors of the sanctuary and the savor of the beauty of the house. I present you with the thurible of your office. Thanks be to God, my brother, for that true incense which hallows our life.

FRATER THURIFICANS: In the name of our fires of longing, and by the word ******, I assume the thurible of my office and accept the duties which it signifies as a servant of God and my brethren.

The Frater Thurificans passes with the sun to his place in the due west of the temple and takes his seat.

The newly-appointed Frater Aquarius is led to the east and invested.

MASTER OF THE TEMPLE: By the power to me committed, I ordain you Aquarius of this temple until the next festival of the Equinox, to watch over the cup of cleansing water and to purify therewith the brethren of all grades and the Postulants. May you also in your own soul be sprinkled as with hyssop and cleansed. May you be washed and made whiter than snow. I present you with the lavacrum of your office. Thanks be to God, my brother, for that Living Water which cleanses the whole creation.

FRATER AQUARIUS: In the name of the Waters of Salvation, and by the word ******, I receive the lavacrum of my office and accept the duties which it signifies as a servant of God and my brethren.

The Frater Aquarius passes with the sun to his place in the due west of the temple and takes his seat. The Master of the Temple gives a battery of one knock.

MASTER OF THE TEMPLE: To order, Fratres et Sorores. My house is a house of prayer.

All rise and face east.

MASTER OF THE TEMPLE: Renew us, O Master of All, in the sanctity of Thy daily service. Fortify the rites of this temple with the prevention of Thy plenary grace. Make it, we pray Thee, among things that testify below, a type of Thine Eternal Presence. Lift up our hearts therein. Be unto us an indwelling spirit, a glory in the midst thereof. So shall we encompass Thine altar, clothed in the understanding of Thy law, clothed in a robe of splendor, which is the showing forth of Thy will within us. Call us, in fine, from the ministry of Thy sacraments in the world of manifested things to the ineffable world of Thine union. (*And then turning westward, with wand uplifted,*) Fratres et Sorores, by the power to me committed, I proclaim that the sun has entered Aries (*vel Libra*), the sign of the vernal (*vel autumnal*) Equinox. Light from the eternal and glory of everlasting worship be with us forever and ever.

The closing is then taken in the Grade of Neophyte.

HERE ENDS THE SOLEMN CELEBRATION OF THE EQUINOX.

Ceremonies of the Fellowship of the Rosy Cross

The Third Order Of The Rosy Cross

World of the Creation
Part V

The Pontifical Ceremony of
Celebrating the Festivals of the
Winter and Summer Solstice

Pars Prima: Quae Est
Pars Magna Secreta
Mysterium Daath

The arrangement of the house follows the unwritten precedents. The door of the sanctuary is open to its full extent. The High Priest of the sanctuary is discovered within, at the eastern end, in full vestments and regalia. On the circular altar there is placed a chalice containing sacramental wine and covered by a paten, on which is unleavened bread.

A white cloth is laid over these vessels. The Fratres et Sorores of the 7=4 degree are assembled and clothed. Frater Civis Regni Superni, spokesman of the Adepti Exempti, has his seat in front of the brethren, bearing his wand. He gives a battery of one knock.

THE HIGH PRIEST: In the name of the three Supernals: in the Holy and Undivided Name. The Lord is the part of mine inheritance: the Lord is the Bread of Life. He giveth bread to them that fear Him. The Lord is the part of my chalice: He giveth the Chalice of Salvation. The wine is ecstasy, containing in itself all sweetness.

Frater Civis Regni Superni gives a battery of one knock and all rise.

THE HIGH PRIEST: Assist me to open, O Lord, this consecrated temple in the Grade which is above all grades, in the Mystery which has not been declared. I open it as a door in Chesed for the descent of Supernal influences from the Light of the Crown, from the Face of Eternal Beauty, on which all the choirs of sanctity have desired to look from the beginning. I open it as a door for the descent of Divine Influence from Thee, O Father of Wisdom, by Whom the worlds were made, and from Thee, O Mother of Understanding, Holy, Holy Bride. Glory be unto the three Supernals in the place where no evil enters, the place of the Tree of Life. There are three that bear witness in Heaven,

And these three are One. Hereof is the bond of union between all who desire below and all who are blessed above, from henceforth and forever. Glory be unto the three Supernals, glory in the place of peace, praise from the mercy suspiring in Chesed and receiving as a free gift the compassion abiding in Kether, world without end. Glory be unto the three Supernals in the sepulcher of mystical death; and from those who are asleep in Geburah, looking for resurrection in God, be there praise till the day of Renewal. Glory be unto the three Supernals, glory to the Eternal beauty, ever ancient and ever new; glory from the place of the living, the house of the Second Birth and the temple of Tiphereth, the beauty of the life that is in Christ. Daath is an open door and Daath the channel of reflection. Amen. It derives to the Sephiroth below, even unto Thee, O Malkuth. Lift up Thine eyes therefore, Thou Mother in manifestation, because of the redemption that is at hand, and the Light of the Supernals upon Thee through the ages and ages.

He then adds with moving lips, but not in an audible voice:

THE HIGH PRIEST: By the power in me vested, I raise this Fellowship of the Rosy Cross, from the world of benignity in Tiphereth, to the threshold of ineffable mystery, the unseen portal in Daath. *(And then as he raises his hands on high:)*

27

Lift up mine arms, lest they fail, O Jehovah Elohim — Holy Father, Holy Mother. May mine eyes in their desire be lifted up: may I see the supreme crown of Kether and the glory of the first hypostasis.

The High Priest raises the Elements in the sight of the holy assembly: but the veil is still over them. Frater Civis Regni Superni gives a battery of one knock.

FRATER CIVIS REGNI SUPERNI: And Melchizedek King of Salem brought forth bread and wine.

The High Priest uncovers the Elements.

FRATER CIVIS REGNI SUPERNI: And he was the priest of the Most High God.

There is a vessel of consecrated water and there is an aspergillus on the pillar at the northern side of the sanctuary door. On the pillar at the southern side there is a vessel of consecrated fire from which the fume of incense rises. Frater Civis Regni Superni passes to the northern pillar, from which he takes the lavacrum and aspergillus. Following the sun, he goes before the Adepti Exempti, makes the Kabalistic sign of the cross with the aspergillus and sprinkles water thrice.

FRATER CIVIS REGNI SUPERNI: Do Thou purify us, O Lord, from stain, that we may look with our own eyes upon the symbols of Thy great mysteries.

Replacing the vessel of water, he takes the thuribulum from the southern pillar and offers incense in the same manner.

FRATER CIVIS REGNI SUPERNI: With incense from Thine altar which is above, and with Supernal Fire, do Thou consecrate our hearts and our reins, that we may be present when Thy hidden things are declared in the land of the living.

The thuribulum being restored to the southern pillar and Frater Civis Regni Superni having returned to his place:

THE HIGH PRIEST *(speaking henceforth audibly):* Symbols of the Life which is Eternal, be unto us a channel for the communication of Eternal Life.

The High Priest bends his head over the Elements, and there is the pause of a moment. Frater Civis Regni Superni gives a battery of one knock and kneels down, with the Adepti Exempti in the body of the temple.

The High Priest removes the paten from the chalice and having laid it on the altar he extends his hands over the bread.

THE HIGH PRIEST: Be thou seed of the Fruit of Life, and when placed in prepared ground, do thou give increase in due season, even twelve manners of fruit, for the glory in adornment of the garden, for the nourishment of elect nations, the grace of the world to come and the descent of the Kingdom.

He extends his hands over the chalice.

THE HIGH PRIEST: The bond between man and God is the life of the chalice of Salvation. Be thou the sign of that Covenant, an open and plenary channel for the communication of Divine Essence, substance of the world within and Life of the life of man.

There is here the pause of a moment.

THE HIGH PRIEST: The food of angels is in Chesed. That food is too light for our sustenance: give us therefore, O Lord, the wells of nourishment which are concealed in Thy limitless light.

He proceeds to the consecration of the Elements in the terms of the MASS OF UNION, *speaking inaudibly throughout. Thereafter he adds slowly and clearly.*

THE HIGH PRIEST: The bread is the Bread of Heaven: this Bread is Heaven in its sweetness. The wine is the Wine of Heaven: this Wine is ecstasy.

He takes up one of the hosts.

THE HIGH PRIEST: Thou hast drawn me through the gate of death; I have dwelt in the palace of Thy Clemency; I have traversed the path of TETH.

He breaks the host and places one of the particles in the chalice.

THE HIGH PRIEST: The fraction of the body of this world: the mystery of Divine Substance communicated to the soul of man. One thing I have desired in my heart, and that is Thou.

He consumes what remains of the host.

THE HIGH PRIEST: I desire to be dissolved and to be with Thee. The Life of life is Thy union. The mystery of Divine Life communicated to the soul of man.

He partakes of the chalice and then, having bowed his head in recollection for a few moments:

THE HIGH PRIEST: The Lord shall be unto me an everlasting light, and my God shall be my glory.

He replaces the paten on the chalice, and following the sun passes outside the sanctuary to the altar in the middle place of the temple, saying in the course of his progress:

THE HIGH PRIEST: This is the place of the clean oblation; the place is prepared and meet, the temple pure and holy. This is the place of unspotted offerings, the place of the offerings of life. Thrice holy is the temple of Thy service, O Lord, my God, in the life which henceforth and forever is ours, O Father, in Thee, and this the life of resurrection.

31

He has reached the eastern side of the altar. In the meantime, Frater Civis Regni Supemi approaches the Adeptus Exemptus who has been chosen to serve in the temple as Celebrant-in-Chief during the ensuing twelve months, and leads him to the western side of the Altar.   Other Adepti are seated.*

*In the Ceremony of the Summer Solstice it is the Celebrant-in-Chief who comes forward - but without official vestments and insignia - to receive the Elements.

THE HIGH PRIEST: And after years of famine, O brethren of the Rose and Cross, milk in the land and honey, corn in the land and wine. Lift up your hearts therefore, as cups at a feast are lifted. Lift up your branches of myrtle. I am the messenger of the Supernals, and I pronounce separation forever between the good and evil. The Tree of Knowledge becometh the Tree of Life; the grace of the knowledge of goodness filleth the heart entirely.

Frater Civis Regni Superni assists the Celebrant-in-Chief Elect to kneel at the western side of the altar and then resumes his seat.

THE HIGH PRIEST: Who is hungry for the Lord? Who is athirst?

The Celebrant-in-Chief Elect says, with bowed head and clasped hands:

CELEBRANT-IN-CHIEF ELECT: Behold the servant of the Lord, and the servant of the servants of God, in the house of my God and Lord, in His Holy Temple.

THE HIGH PRIEST: That hunger is justice: may the Three Which bear witness in Heaven deal with you in Eternal Justice and feed you.

The High Priest lifts up one of the hosts and places it in the mouth of the Celebrant-in-Chief Elect, who raises his head to receive it and again bows it.

THE HIGH PRIEST: That thirst is righteousness. May you gather grapes in living vineyards and tread the wine-press of Salvation. May the Keeper of the Eternal Vineyard bring you Wine of Life in great flagons, in cups running over.

The Celebrant-in-Chief Elect raises his head; the chalice is placed to his lips and he drinks thereof. Again he bows his head. The Priest replaces the paten on the chalice and covers them with the white cloth. *

In the Ceremony of the Summer Solstice, the Celebrant-In-Chief goes back to his place; the High Priest returns directly to the sanctuary and proceeds with the work therein.

THE HIGH PRIEST: Frater Electus ex Millibus (*vel nomen aliud*), merciful and Exempt Adept, like other graduates in the house of the Holy Spirit and its school of sanctity, you have gone forth in search of that light which enters into the heart of those who have put aside the burden of their birth according to the will of flesh and the will of man, that they might be reborn in God. You have followed the life of rebirth, which is also a life of crucifixion in respect of all that is below. In the sleep of mystical death, you have realized the Divine within by a union at the center, as a marriage with the Life of life.

In the glorious mysteries of resurrection, you have entered into the Life of union, which is wedded life in God. By these and all other memorials of your everlasting spirit, I bid you arise, my brother (*the High Priest leans across the Altar, takes him by the two hands and raises him*), as one who is clothed in peace, and the Light of the Supernals be upon you forever and ever.

I commission and warrant you to represent in the Third Order of the Rosy Cross the ineffable mercy of God toward those who are called to partake in this temple and sanctuary of the mysteries which lead into salvation.

Bring those who have been prepared and consecrated in the lower grades of the Fellowship by a straight and narrow path to the portal of Tiphereth. So shall you reach down into Netzach and draw all things after you from Yesod. Bring them into the sanctuary of adepts, that they may hear the Divine Voice speaking of the Divine in the universe and the self-knowing spirit testifying concerning itself and the mystery of attainment in Christ.

Give unto them their sleep in Geburah and after the ecstasy of union do thou raise them in the glory of Chesed. Salutation and peace and joy, all grace and holiness of heart, be with you now and henceforward during the twelve months' work of your office. So let your light be extended in the heaven of this holy temple that you may be worthy to depart in peace at the end of your stewardship.

The Celebrant-in-Chief Elect says, with crossed arms:

CELEBRANT-IN-CHIEF ELECT: I go forth in the power of thy warrant, carrying the tidings of salvation and the living symbols of the Word.

The High Priest returns direct to the sanctuary and there facing west at the eastern side of the interior altar, he says with outstretched arms and open hands:

THE HIGH PRIEST: The Light of the Supernals be upon you, the grace of the Supernals enter and abide in your hearts, with the blessing of all blessings, leading through the knowledge of goodness to Divine understanding, the sum of wisdom and the glorious crown of life.

There is here the pause of a moment.

THE HIGH PRIEST: By the power in me vested, I close this holy temple in the Grade which is above all grades, in the Mystery which has not been declared.

And then with moving lips only:

THE HIGH PRIEST: In the name of the Three Supernals, in the Holy and Undivided Name, I who am the priest of Daath, at the sacred portal thereof, do restore this Third Order of the Rosy Cross — Chesed, Geburah and Tiphereth — from the threshold of ineffable mystery to its proper place in the first reflected triad.

The Celebrant Elect returns to his seat. The High Priest passes with the sun through the door of the sanctuary, which he closes behind him. He takes his proper place in the body of the temple.

Here ends the mystery of Daath.

PARS SECUNDA: MYSTERIUM CHESED

The Temple is opened in full according to the ritual of the Grade of Adeptus Exemptus by the Celebrant-in-Chief and the Most Holy Priestess. The Fratres et Sorores are seated. The Usher of the Grade goes to the eastern side of the altar and there lifts up his wand.

FRATER CIVIS REGNI SUPERNI: Summer and winter shall not cease. Fratres et Sorores, merciful and Exempt Adepts, I proclaim the high festival of the Winter (*vel Summer)* Solstice.

He returns to his place.

ADEPTUS EXEMPTUS: The house of the Holy Spirit is open in the grade of Chesed for the commemoration of the event and the celebration of the Sacred Mysteries attached thereto.* Give me grace, O Lord, to end my task in peace, that - having been manifested in the mystical body of this life which I draw from Thee - I may pass into the hidden refuge of Thy more perfect union. I have served Thee, my King and God, in those grades of salvation by which the Fellowship of the Rosy Cross is bound upon the Tree of Life. I have drawn those whom Thou hast given me from the deeps below Malkuth. I have brought them from the sphere of Yesod, by a straight way, to the portal of the Third Order, and thence into the life of the cross. I have put them to rest in Geburah, and at the end I have raised them gloriously when Easter dawned in their souls. Set upon my forehead the seal of Thine unchanging simplicity. Bid me go inward. Take me to the still rest of the Active Center, into the World of Ascension in Daath.

In the ceremony of the Summer Solstice the speech of the Celebrant-in-Chief ends at this point, with the addition of the following words: "The life of resurrection is the solstice of eternal summer." He puts aside his wand and proceeds to the western end of the altar, facing east. The High Priest, rising in his place and standing thereat, inquires: "Whence come thou, Frater Dilectissime?" The ceremony proceeds as in the text above, with the answer to this question, and after reciting the thrice-great Pledge of Fidelity, the Celebrant re-

turns to his seat, resumes his wand, and the closing is taken forthwith in the grade of Adeptus Exemptus.

THE PRIESTESS: Frater Civis Regni Superni, where is the faithful witness who shall testify in the coming time?

The Usher of the Grade proceeds with the sun to the place of the Celebrant Elect, whom he brings to the western side of the altar, looking toward the east, and returns to his own place.

ADEPTUS EXEMPTUS: Art thou he that is to come, or do we look for another?

THE CELEBRANT ELECT: O Adepti Exempti, in virtue of the warrants which I carry, receive the perfect signs.

He gives the sign of a Neophyte.

THE CELEBRANT ELECT: The sign of him who, standing on the threshold of the path, bears witness to the mystery of the Tree.

He gives the sign of a Zelator.

THE CELEBRANT ELECT: The sign of him who, passing between the pillars, receives the blessing of the quest.

He gives the sign of a Frater Theoreticus.

THE CELEBRANT ELECT: The sign of him who enters the path of attainment, and the mystery of the Tree of Life is rooted in his part of mind.

He gives the sign of a Practicus.

THE CELEBRANT ELECT: The sign of him whose heart is in the holy quest and the Tree of Life is rooted in the heart of him.

He gives the sign of a Philosophus.

THE CELEBRANT ELECT: The sign of him in whom the Tree of Life overshadows the whole personality and the will of his inmost being is directed to the end in God.

He gives the sign of an Adeptus Minor.

THE CELEBRANT ELECT: The sign of Messias extended on the Tree of Life, and the sign of the Christ Mystical abiding in the life of the heart.

He gives the sign of an Adeptus Major.

THE CELEBRANT ELECT: The sign of the inward state of him who has died in Christ, of the soul dissolved in the spirit by an ecstasy of love, of the Word quickened in the soul by the central realization thereof.

The Most Holy Priestess rises from her seat between the pil-

lars, passes about the altar and faces the Celebrant Elect from the eastern side.

The Celebrant Elect gives the sign of an Adeptus Exemptus.

THE CELEBRANT ELECT: The sign of resurrection in Christ, of the Word manifest in risen life and expounding the mystery of the Tree.

The Most Holy Priestess and the Celebrant Elect exchange the grip of the grade of Chesed across the altar.

THE PRIESTESS: The perfect testimony of perfect signs is given and received, O brother of the Rosy Cross.

She returns to her place.

ADEPTUS EXEMPTUS: Whence come you, Frater Dilectissime?

THE CELEBRANT ELECT: I have been in search of my spirit through the ages. I have reached the term of quest. I have come with the glad tidings, to bear my faithful witness in all the holy houses of the Rosy Cross.

ADEPTUS EXEMPTUS: What manner of glad tidings, O merciful and Exempt Adept?

THE CELEBRANT ELECT: Tidings of the trinity which enters into unity, of attainment in self-knowing spirit, of ineffable union in spirit, soul and flesh. I testify concerning the deep things of experience declared in the way of truth, seeing that the work of redemption devolves on those who have sought and obtained redemption. On my own part, and as vicegerent and spokesman of all Adepti Exempti under the obedience of this Rite, I look to carry unto the bounds and ends of the mystical earth my glad tidings concerning the glorious resurrection of Adeptship to the new life which is hidden and manifested in God. So far as I may fail in this high and holy task, may my peers and coheirs concur with myself in atonement, that nothing may be stinted or restricted of that which has been put into my charge, so only that the prescribed order is maintained duly and that which belongs to the sanctuary is reserved thereto. Hereof is the faithful witness of every Exempt Adept in the grade of Chesed.

The High Priest rises and passes to the eastern side of the cubical altar in the middle place of the temple.

THE HIGH PRIEST: Frater Electus ex millibus (*vel nomen aliud*), before the altar in this house of the Lord there must be a pledge between us and you, and God shall watch upon the covenant forever. May that which we do in your person, collectively and individually, be ratified in Daath, wherein is the life of ascension; and the power of the Supernals attest it forever and ever. I say unto you, lift up your hands, and the testimony which I utter on my own part in the fullness of the manifested Word, you shall now recite not only in the secret soul and the inmost heart but with the lips of him whose mouth is opened in the grade of Exempt Adept.

The Usher of the Grade gives a battery of one knock and all rise. The High Priest imposes the thrice great Pledge of Fidelity, and it is repeated by the Celebrant Elect. The High Priest returns to his place, and the brethren are seated. While still standing at the altar:

ADEPTUS EXEMPTUS: May he that comes after me so work and so achieve that he shall be preferred before me and that the latchet of his shoes I shall be called unworthy to loose.

THE CELEBRANT ELECT: O Lord and Master of all, vouchsafe to look with pity on these Adepti Exempti, exalted and merciful, who are placed in my charge for the sacred and glorious offices of this hidden temple devoted to Thy service. May that which is here and now to them ascribed in symbolism be effectually and really imparted; and may those whom I bring during the term of my office into the mysteries of the grade of Chesed be integration in the Life of the Tree, by the dispensation of Thy Divine Mercy.

The Celebrant Elect returns to his seat,

The Closing is taken in the grade of Adeptus Exemptus. Here ends the Mystery of Chesed.

Pars Tertia: Mysterium Geburah

The Adepti Majores are admitted. The temple is opened in full according to the Ritual of the Grade of Adeptus Major by the Celebrants of that grade. The Fratres et Sorores are seated. The Usher of the Grade goes to the eastern side of the altar and there lifts up his wand.

Frater Peregrinus Vallis: Summer and winter shall not cease. Fratres et Sorores, Adepti Majores, I proclaim the high festival of the Winter (*vel Summer*) Solstice.

He returns to his place.

Adeptus Exemptus: The house of the Holy Spirit is open in the grade of Geburah for the commemoration of the event and the celebration of the Sacred Mysteries attached thereto.* I have watched for more than one hour in the vigil of holy souls. The day has been given me for labor; the night remains for contemplation; and both are offices of love. Give unto me henceforth, O Lord, more perfect knowledge of Thy love in the ineffable wonder of Thy silence. I have brought those whom Thou hast given me from the world of regenerated life to a portal that opens on the center, to the valley of mystical darkness and the union of souls therein. O Lord, my task is done. Remember Thy Sabbath and the promise of that narrow path which leads to the crown. I desire to put off mortality and to be clothed in Thee.

* In the ceremony of the Summer Solstice the speech of the Celebrant-In-Chief ends at this point. The Second Celebrant puts aside his wand and proceeds to the western end of the altar, facing east. The High Priest, rising in his place and standing thereat, inquires: "Whence come thou, Frater Dilectissime?" *The Ceremony proceeds as in the text above, omitting the address of the Adeptus Exemptus beginning:* "Merciful Exempt Adept, my peer and successor" - *and the grip being exchanged between the Second and First Celebrant, who goes to the eastern side of the altar for this purpose, and then returns to his place. Thereafter the High Priest imposes the obligation of the grade on the Second Celebrant. At the end they return to their places, the Adeptus Major resumes his wand, and the closing is taken forthwith in plenary form.*

ADEPTUS MAJOR: Frater Peregrinus Vallis, where is the faithful witness on whom the task devolves?

The Usher of the Grade proceeds with the sun to the place of the Celebrant Elect, whom he brings to the western side of the altar, looking toward the east, and returns to his place.

ADEPTUS EXEMPTUS: Art thou he that is to come, or do we look for another?

THE CELEBRANT ELECT: O Adepti Majores, in virtue of the warrants which I carry, receive the sacred testimony. I have cast out the images of matter, the illusory testimony of the senses, the lust of the flesh, the lust of the eyes and the pride of life. I have put away the desires of the body. I have cast out the symbols of the mind: I have set aside the desires thereof. The end has dawned in the silence. The emotions of the soul are transmuted; the desire of human will is absorbed in the purpose of God. The spirit and the soul are one: the life of the soul is hidden with Christ in God.

ADEPTUS MAJOR: Hereof is the mystery that we celebrate. Be it given unto him who thus puts off mortality to assume the Body of Christ.

ADEPTUS EXEMPTUS: Whence come you, Frater Dilectissime?

THE CELEBRANT ELECT: From the house of Love and of the soul going to its bridal; from a temple of holy espousals; from a place of peace, and there is the voice of the silence; from a world within, stilled in the waters of contemplation - and these are waters of Love. I have known the mystic union of the Lover and Beloved. I come forth with the glad tidings, and I will bear my faithful witness in the holy temples.

ADEPTUS MAJOR: What manner of glad tidings, O traveler in the valley of death ?

THE CELEBRANT ELECT: Tidings of ineffable experience which lies within the mystery of death, of the light within which exceeds all light without, and the coming of the Peacemaker. I have heard the call of the union, the still small voice speaking in the heart of longing, and the Center has drawn me back. I testify that the Eternal God is imminent in creation, as a Great Architect hidden within a sanctuary of His own building. I testify to the Divine imminent in the soul of man and that the Divine awakens within it. O wanderers in the valley of silence, keepers of the halls of Geburah, watchers in the rock-hewn sepulcher, I have known the sanctity of death beyond the setting sun. As vicegerent and spokesman, I testify on your part and on that of Adepti Majores wherever assembled under the obedience of this rite, that - God willing - we desire to be dissolved and henceforth to abide in Him. May I on my own part be uplifted into the Divine Purpose, that all whom I commend in this grade into the hands of God may be united with the living power of the Word and the Light thereof. Whenever He shall call, I will enter the great mystery imploring peace upon the world. Hereof is the faithful witness of every Adeptus Major in the grade of Geburah.

Adeptus Exemptus: Merciful Exempt Adept, my peer and my successor, go forth in the power of your warrant and complete this high ceremony of the Winter (*vel Summer*) Solstice, that when the Holy Order of the Rosy Cross is withdrawn for one moment of time from the World of Regenerated Life in the grade of Tiphereth, it may be formulated once more in beauty.

The Celebrants rise and exchange the grip of the grade with the Celebrant Elect.

Adeptus Major: Yod, He

ADEPTUS EXEMPTUS: The union of Jehovah and Elohim, of God and His Shekinah in Kether.

The Celebrants return to their places. The Usher of the Grade leads the Celebrant Elect to the door of the sanctuary and causes him to turn westward. He then goes back to his place. The High Priest comes forward and faces the Celebrant Elect.

THE HIGH PRIEST: Frater Electus ex millibus (*vel nomen aliud*), before the sanctuary in this house of the Lord there must be a pledge between us and you, and God shall watch upon the covenant forever. May that which we do in your person, collectively and individually, be ratified in Chesed, wherein is the life of Resurrection; and the power of the Supernals, attest it forever and ever. So stand therefore, my brother, with arms extended in the sacred cruciform sign, and say in your heart of hearts that which you utter with your lips.

The Usher of the Grade gives a battery of one knock and all rise. The High Priest imposes the sacrament of the holy pledge. Thereafter he returns to his place and the brethren are seated. While still standing before the door of the sanctuary:

THE CELEBRANT ELECT: O Lord and Master of all, vouchsafe to look with pity on these mighty Adepti Majores, who are placed in my charge for the sacred and glorious offices of our hidden temple, dedicated to Thy service. May that which

47

is here and now to them ascribed in symbolism be effectually and really imparted; and may those whom I shall bring during my term of office into the mysteries of the grade of Geburah be integrated in the Life of the Tree, by the dispensation of Thine all-merciful judgment.

He opens the door of the sanctuary, enters therein and shuts the door behind him.

The closing is then taken in the grade of Adeptus Major. Here ends the mystery of Geburah.

Pars Quarta: Mysterium Tiphereth

The arrangement of the temple follows the unwritten precedents. The Auxiliary Frater Adeptus assumes his vestments and insignia. The Honorable Frater Custos Liminis has charge of a Thurible, from which incense rises. The Celebrants repair to their places. The lights of the Temple are extinguished, with the exception of three candles burning on the Altar and symbolising the Offices of the Celebrants. The Adcpti Minores are admitted and take their seats. As Usher of the Grade, the Honorable Frater Custos Liminis goes to the Eastern side of the Circular Altar and there uplifts his Wand.

Frater Custos Liminis: Summer and Winter shall not cease. Fratres et Sorores, Adepti Minores, I proclaim the High Festival of the Winter Solstice. *(If Summer, see appended Ceremony for Summer Solstice)*

Adeptus Exemptus: The house of the Holy Spirit is open in the grade of Tiphereth for the commemoration of the event and the celebration of the sacred mysteries attached thereto. It is opened in darkness for the office of a sacred watch, awaiting the Light of the Word and the Glory of the Lord manifested in this temple devoted to His service by the Fellowship of the Rosy Cross.

The Usher of the Grade returns to his proper place.

Adeptus Major: Quench not the light of Israel in the withdrawing thereof.

Auxiliary Frater Adeptus: He bringeth out to light from the darkness, even the shadow of death.

Adeptus Major: When the Chief Shepherd shall appear, may we receive a crown of glory that fadeth not away.

Auxiliary Frater Adeptus: He shall be as the light of the morning, even a morning without clouds.

Adeptus Major: This shall be the day of our deliverance, Thy day, O Lord and Master, the day of saving grace, wherein all things shall be renewed.

49

Auxiliary Frater Adeptus: Set an end, O Lord, to the darkness, and let not Thine order be suspended.

Adeptus Exemptus: Below is the darkness of material things; above is the light of the Spirit; between them are the gifts and the graces which are manifested by the Spirit in the heights to the soul awakening in man. Below is the reflected light of the lesser mysteries, comprised by the lower grades of the Rosy Cross; above are the greater mysteries; between them lies the regenerated life of Tiphereth, beneath the everlasting wings of the Holy One, looking toward Divine experience in the mystic death of the Adept, and thereafter to the Life of Resurrection, when the Spirit of Christ within shall rule our consecrated elements.

Auxiliary Frater Adeptus: We have watched in all grades of the Order, expecting Thy coming, because of Thy most sure promises. We gave our bodies to Thy service in the consecrations of the Sephira Malkuth, and Thy reflected light shone through the kingdom below. The Shekinah testified concerning Thee, and the vestiges of grace from the crown fed us at holy tables. Thy house is a house of prayer, but the spirit of this world had made it a den of thieves. In the hope of Thy coming we cast out from the temple of Mind those traffickers in wares that have no part on Thine altars. Our temple was filled with constant thought of Thee. The shadow of Thy Presence abode therein; and a sacred fear that is the beginning of wisdom inspired us in the Sephira Yesod, as in a Holy of Holies. But it was surely Thine own voice over the troubled sea of emotion, passion and desire of the heart, which uttered that: Peace, be still; and a quiet like the perfect end fell upon the flux of the soul. A glory like Thy glory was declared in the Sephira Hod. We believed that the time was nigh, even at the doors; and we made ready for Thine advent in Netzach, where the will within us turned to Thy Holy ends. Thereafter a way was opened to the second birth of being and the life of regeneration in Tiphereth, where all Thy speaking symbols testify by true signs concerning Thy Presence. May the high light shine in our souls and the spirit prophesy within. May we know Thee, O Christ, within and be nourished by Thy Divine Substance, wherein is life everlasting.

ADEPTUS EXEMPTUS: May the day of expectation be also the day of union, and in this house of the Holy Spirit give unto us reintegration in Thee.

The Auxiliary Frater Adeptus rises and draws near to the altar on the eastern side. He lifts up the light attributed to his office in the altar symbolism and, raising it to his forehead, circumambulates the temple slowly, pausing at the four quarters.

AUXILIARY FRATER ADEPTUS *(at the south.):* I know that my Redeemer liveth and that He shall stand at the latter day upon the earth. *(At the west.)* He will redeem us with stretched out arm and with great judgments. *(At the north.)* We have remembered that God is our rock, and the High God is our Redeemer. *(He returns to the east, which he faces.)* In the soul's famine, He shall redeem the soul from death; He shall redeem it from the grave; He shall draw nigh unto the soul and save it; He shall save the souls of His servants, *(He turns westward.)* O Lord, Thou hast pleaded the cause of our souls; Thou hast ransomed our life. All flesh shall know the Savior. Blessed be the Lord Who hath not left us this day without a Redeemer.

He returns to the altar and there extinguishes his light, saying:

Auxiliary Frater Adeptus: I desire to be dissolved and to be with Christ.

He replaces his extinguished light on the Altar and goes direct to his seat, where he lays down his official vestments and insignia. He stands now at his seat, facing west.

Auxiliary Frater Adeptus: As a vesture shalt Thou change us and we shall be changed. I have assumed vestments for Thy glory; I put them off for Thy praise. Give me in Thine own good time the whole armor of salvation.

He moves round the altar with the sun and takes his place in the body of the temple, among unofficial Adepti Minores.

Adeptus Major: Thou hast made us in the likeness of the universe, as a garden that is entered at birth, and we have found in Thy high consecrations a secret door which opens from earthly into spiritual life, as a paradise of the soul within. We have dwelt in Thy light in that garden and the second birth in Thee has sanctified all its ways. The growth of nature becometh the growth of grace. The earth is the root of that kingdom which cometh from heaven above; the air is a breath of paradise; the rain that waters the garden is the life-giving rain of love, and the rays of the sun that warms it are rays of Thy Divine Life. But in the garden, O Master of all, we have found another and more secret door, which leads from regenerated life to a mystical death at the center. In the valley of the shadows, in the underworld of being, give unto those who desire Thee the blessed victory of death, the vision of the dark night, the mystery of union therein and the eternal Word of Life.

Adeptus Exemptus: If a man shall keep this testimony alive in the temple of his heart, he shall not see death for ever. May neither death nor life divide us from Thy love, O God.

The Adeptus Major rises and draws near to the altar on its eastern side. He lifts up the light attributed to his office in the altar symbolism and, raising it to his forehead, circumambulates the temple slowly, pausing at the four quarters.

Adeptus Major *(at the south.):* I have commended my soul into Thy hands, O God. *(At the west.)* It shall be given me to see Thee outside the flesh of my body; I shall see Thee and no other: I shall behold Thee with mine eyes. *(At the north.)* I am least among the sons of election, but I have gone down into the valley of shadows, to be judged in Thy Love therein. *(He returns to the east, which he faces.)* I have seen Thee in the valley of vision. Thy light was upon all the ways. I was safe under the covert of Thy wings in the mystic tomb. Thou hast opened fountains in the midst of the valleys. *(He turns westward.)* I have been through the inmost distance and through the great deep. In peace; in that I have slept and I have rested.

He returns to the altar and there extinguishes his light, saying:

ADEPTUS MAJOR: Thou shalt deliver our souls and our life shall see Thy light. Do Thou enlighten us with the light of the living.

He replaces his extinguished light on the altar and goes directly to his seat, where he lays down his official vestments and insignia. He stands now at his seat, facing west.

ADEPTUS MAJOR: Thy priests are clothed with salvation; Thy saints rejoice in goodness. Blessed is he that watcheth and keepeth his garments. When the Lord unclothes him, the same shall give true account of his stewardship. Clothe me, O Master, in Thy good time with the perfect body of resurrection.

He moves round the altar with the sun and takes his place in the Temple among unofficial Adepti Majores. The sole light in the temple is that which is attributed to the office of Celebrant-in-Chief, who now rises in his place and his seat is removed.

ADEPTUS EXEMPTUS: Fratres et Sorores of the Fellowship of the Rosy Cross, in the covenant of everlasting priesthood, I leave my spirit with you in those who come after me.

He turns eastward. The Usher of the Grade gives a battery of one knock and all rise.

ADEPTUS EXEMPTUS: Thou hast given us many deliverers and many precursors of salvation, and Thou hast permitted even me to testify in the symbolism of this Thy holy temple concerning Thine advent. My task is done. I came in Thy Name, O Lord. Do Thou come in Thine own with power, or send him whom Thou willest to maintain the faithful witness. I am called to go inward. Lord, now lettest Thou Thy servant depart in peace. In the opening of the path of Yod, I return whence I came. *(He now faces west.)* The peace of God be with you, O brethren of the Rosy Cross; and be He realized within you Who is all days with us, even to the consummation of the world.

The Celebrant-in-Chief removes his official vestments and insignia, which are received by the Usher of the Grade, who comes up for this purpose, and having laid them on the seat of the Celebrant he returns to his place.

ADEPTUS EXEMPTUS: Thou hast compassed me with holy garments. I lay down those which I have worn in the temple of Thy service. I would put off all mortal clothing and receive that which is immortal, confessing Thy Name, O God, in the unity of Supernal knowledge. Cover me with Thy light, as with a garment.

The Celebrant-in-Chief draws near to the altar on its eastern side. He lifts up the light attributed to his office in the altar symbolism and, turning eastward, passes to the door of the sanctuary, which he sets open and pauses upon the threshold.

The sanctuary is in utter darkness. The cross of obligation is in the center thereof, and the Celebrant-in-Chief Elect is on his knees before it, his head bowed deeply.

The High Priest stands at the eastern end, with extended arms.

THE HIGH PRIEST: I will raise me up a faithful priest, who shall do according to that which is in mine heart and in my mind: and he shall walk before mine anointed forever.

The outgoing Celebrant enters the sanctuary and stands at the northern side of the cross, bearing his light. The High Priest comes round to the southern side and bends over the Celebrant Elect.

THE HIGH PRIEST: The Son of Man cometh not to receive ministry but to minister, wearing in humility the likeness of the Lord of Glory.

He raises the Celebrant Elect, saying:

THE HIGH PRIEST: It is written: He that taketh not his cross, and followeth after me, is not worthy of me.

He places him against the cross and comes forward to the door of the sanctuary.

THE HIGH PRIEST: He that is greatest among you, let him be as the younger, and he that is Chief as he that doth serve.

He turns to the Celebrant Elect.

THE HIGH PRIEST: That the world may be crucified unto thee, do thou crucify thyself unto the world.

The Celebrant Elect extends his arms upon the cross.

THE CELEBRANT ELECT: I am made and vowed as you are, and the burden of your dedication is upon me, that I shall not leave you in the heat of the day or in the hour of trial, but that I may give an account of my stewardship. I testify concerning myself, that you may bear witness in turn. On behalf of you who are my brethren, I set myself upon the cross of obligation, to renew my pledges and your own in the presence of the whole Order.

The High Priest binds the Celebrant Elect to the cross.

THE HIGH PRIEST: May that which we do in thy person, collectively and individually, on this sacred day of our renewal, be ratified in Geburah, wherein is the victory of death; be it recorded in Chesed, wherein is the life of resurrection; and the power of the Supernals attest it forever and ever.

He administers the obligation of the Grade of Adeptus Minor to the Celebrant Elect, by whom it is repeated audibly. Thereafter, the brethren having resumed their seats and the Celebrant Elect being still bound upon the Cross:

THE CELEBRANT ELECT: May the brethren of this Holy Order be confirmed and strengthened in me. May they die to themselves with me in the lower part of their nature. May they descend with me from the glorious cross of Tiphereth and pass to the ineffable experience of the greater mysteries. As I give expression for testimony in the whole personality of Adepti Minores under the obedience of this sacred rite, so may its high end be realized in them and so also in me. May I thus - who am uplifted on the cross - draw all who are mine unto me. Into Thy hands, O Lord, for this Thy work in the Order, I commend the will of my spirit in the uttermost conformity.

He bows his head.

The Usher of the Grade comes forward and closes the door of the sanctuary. The body of the temple is now in complete darkness. The High Priest unbinds the Celebrant Elect.

THE HIGH PRIEST: Descend, O merciful Exempt Adept, from the glorious cross of Tiphereth, for the deliverance of the souls of the just from earthly into spiritual life, from places of purification to the place of the Second Birth and from the life of regeneration in God to the risen life which is in Him.

The outgoing Celebrant hands the light to his successor.

THE OUTGOING CELEBRANT: May peace be with thee, brother, and do thou carry the tidings of peace.

While this has taken place in the sanctuary, the Usher of the Grade, standing at his place in the body of the temple, repeats the versicles of the time.

FRATER CUSTOS LIMINIS: (1) Let Thy messenger appear in his place. (2) He shall sit as a priest upon his throne. (3) The counsel of his peace shall be upon us. (4) He shall be as the light of morning, when the sun riseth, even a morning without clouds. (5) Come quickly therefore, we pray thee: enter into our hearts and lives, the promised Deliverer.

While these versicles are recited slowly and clearly, the High Priest and the Outgoing Celebrant have issued from the sanctuary by a secret door at the further end. The former takes up his place at the south-west angle of the sanctuary on its outer side and the latter occupies any vacant seat in the body of the temple. All this is done quietly, so that they may not be distinguished in the darkness.

A great light shines within the sanctuary.

FRATER CUSTOS LIMINIS: I have loved Thee, O Lord, my Priest and King of my salvation. Great things are spoken of the Kingdom, because of Thy day.

The battery of the 5=6 grade is sounded within the sanctuary (knocks three times, pauses, knocks twice.) It is repeated by the Usher of the Grade as spokesman of Adepti Minores. The Celebrant-in-Chief comes forth from the sanctuary carrying the light of his office. All lights in the body of the temple are turned on at the same moment. All present rise up. The Celebrant-in-Chief deposits his light on the altar. The High Priest comes forward and places the New Celebrant at a middle point between the sanctuary and the altar, still facing east. The vestments and insignia of the Celebrant are brought up by the Usher of the Grade, who hands them successively to the High Priest and assists generally at the clothing.

THE HIGH PRIEST (*investing with the violet habit):* Wash thee in the heart and anoint thee in the spirit. (*Investing with the violet cloak.)* Put the raiment of thy redeemed body upon thee. (*Investing with the Rose-Cross.)* It is written: I will clothe my priests with salvation. (*Investing with the biretta.)* The saints shall shout for joy. (*Placing the wand of office in the hands of the Celebrant, and then turning westward.)* Who is this that cometh from Edom, with dyed garments from Bozrah? This that is glorious in his apparel, manifesting in the greatness of his strength?

The High Priest returns to his place and resumes his seat, as also the Usher of the Grade and the unofficial brethren. The

Celebrant draws near to the altar on its eastern side. He lifts up the light of his office and, raising it to his forehead, circumambulates the temple slowly, pausing at the four quarters.

Adeptus Exemptus (at the south.): Behold, there is no void, and I testify that there is no distance between God and the soul of man, for the soul that returns to God. *(At the west.)* The yoke of the law is lifted, as an halter taken from the neck. *(At the north.)* The freedom of the Gospel is the liberation of the soul therein. *(At the east.)* To Thy Glory, O God, and the keeping of Thy ways inviolate. *(And then facing west.)* To the glory of the Rosy Cross, and the light of the Lord therein.

He replaces his light on the altar and goes to his proper seat.

ADEPTUS EXEMPTUS: I call upon the Honorable Frater Experimentum Mirabile *(vel nomen aliud),* who has been chosen by the Headship of the Third Order to receive at my hands the benefit of installation in the office of Adeptus Major.

The brother thus cited is brought up by the Usher of the Grade, who assists also in the clothing.

ADEPTUS EXEMPTUS: Frater Experimentum Mirabile *(vel nomen aliud),* as one who is destined to fulfill the sacred duties of mighty Adeptus Major during the coming revolution of the sun, you are held - symbolically speaking - to have been warranted from the grade of Geburah; but Geburah is asleep in the Lord and its rest is not broken. By the power to me committed in the height of the Third Order, and as a Merciful Exempt Adept, I give you your titles from Chesed hereby and herein. Receive the vestments of your office. (*He rises and clothes the Adeptus Major.*) I have put righteousness upon you, and it shall clothe you. Receive also your lamina. When you carry it in the great rites, remember that the death of the cross is truly the gate of Life. I present you with the wand of your office. The cross returns into the cube, the Word made flesh is hidden in the rock-hewn sepulcher, and our life is withdrawn in God.

The Adeptus Major passes to the altar and lights his symbolical candle from that of the Celebrant-in-Chief, who then leads him to his proper seat, and resumes his own.

ADEPTUS EXEMPTUS: I call upon the Honorable Frater Lux semper in Coelis *(vel nomen aliud),* who has been chosen by the Headship of the Third Order to receive at my hands the benefit of installation in the office of Auxiliary Frater Adeptus.

The brother thus cited is brought up by the Usher of the Grade, who assists also in his clothing.

ADEPTUS EXEMPTUS: Frater Lux semper in Ccelis *(vel nomen aliud),* your warrant is delivered in Tiphereth, but it derives from the source of authority which rules and teaches in Chesed. Hereby and herein I proclaim your lawful titles.

Receive the vestments of your office. (*He rises and clothes the Auxiliary Frater Adeptus.*) May your raiment be as light about you and as gold shining in the Sun. May you spread your vestments in the way when the Lord of Hosts comes. Receive also your lamina, and when you carry it in the Great Rite of Tiphereth, remember that the life of the cross is the way of the mystery of God. I present you with the wand of your office. It proclaims that the Word is made flesh and manifested in human life.

The Auxiliary Frater Adeptus passes to the altar, where he lights his symbolical candle from that of the Celebrant-in-Chief, who then leads him to his proper seat and resumes his own. The Usher of the Grade closes the sanctuary. The temple is opened in full in the Grade of Adeptus Minor. Thereafter the three Celebrants remain standing in their proper places.

THE HIGH PRIEST: Raise up, we beseech Thee, O Master of all our ways, the spiritual life of this Order: lift it into the life which is eternal. May the power and the grace and the glory of Thy Most Holy Spirit remain in this house of the Spirit. May all profanation of evil and the hands of the unconsecrated keep far from our sanctuary and its precincts. May those who enter herein be those who are born for the light, and may the high light abide within them - a witness in the soul and the heart. So shall we dwell in Thy presence, in the sanctity of regenerated life, in the liberation of our sleep in Thee, and in the peace of the world to come, which is the world of the Holy One, the world of Resurrection in Thee and of union with Christ the Spirit.

The Celebrant-in-Chief passes to the eastern side of the altar and uncovers the sacred vessels. He lifts up the paten and says:

ADEPTUS EXEMPTUS: Give unto us Divine Substance - communicated to the soul of man.

He lifts up the chalice and says:

ADEPTUS EXEMPTUS: Give unto us Divine Life for the maintenance of the soul in Thee.

Under the guidance of the Usher of the Grade, acting as director of ceremonies, the Fratres et Sorores come forward, beginning with the Official Adepti, the High Priest excepted.

The paten is passed round and they partake of the Hosts, each repeating the sacred formula. The paten is replaced on the altar. The chalice is also passed round, and the brethren drink thereof, repeating the sacred formula. The chalice is replaced on the altar and the Elements are reveiled. The Usher of the Grade is the last to partake of each. The Celebrants return to their thrones. All present having resumed their seats, the High Priest rises in his place.

THE HIGH PRIEST: The Life of life is Thy love. It is written: Behold, I am with you all days, even to the consummation of the world. I have descended to Tiphereth, bringing the glad tidings. *(He lifts up his arms.)* The peace of God and the knowledge of life everlasting, and the consciousness of the self-knowing part in the Eternal Spirit, be with you, world without end.

The altar is replaced in the vault.

ADEPTUS EXEMPTUS: Honorable Fratres et Sorores, by the power to me committed, I proclaim that the sun has entered Capricorn (*vel Cancer*), the sign of the Winter (*vel Summer*) Solstice. Light from the Eternal and Glory of Everlasting Worship be with us forever and ever.

The closing is then taken in the grade of Adeptus Minor.

Here ends the mystery of Tiphereth and Here ends the Solemn Ceremony of Celebrating the Festival of the Winter (vel Summer) Solstice.

Ceremony of Summer Solstice in the Grade of Tiphereth

The temple is opened in the light according to the ritual of the 5=6 grade. The Frater Custos Liminis proclaims the solstice, and the Celebrant-in-Chief proceeds as follows:

ADEPTUS EXEMPTUS: The house of the Holy Spirit is opened in the grade of Tiphereth for the commemoration of the event and the celebration of the sacred mysteries attached thereto. The sun at its greatest elevation is an external type or foreshadowing of the Christ Life in the soul at the highest realization of spiritual consciousness. It is the day of our attainment, Thy day, O Lord and Master, wherein all things are renewed. It is the noonday splendor of the sun of righteousness, the kingdom, the power and the glory. The counsel is: Stand therefore in the fullness of the light, as the sun stands at the zenith.

ADEPTUS MAJOR: The Festival of the Winter Solstice commemorates the advent of the Christ of Palestine, but especially the beginning of the three years of ministry. It commemorates the coming also of the cosmic Christ into the heart of the Rosy Cross. This is the opening of the mysteries, and the light shineth in darkness.

AUXILIARY FRATER ADEPTUS: The Festival of the Summer Solstice commemorates the fullness of manifestation in Palestine, when the risen Christ sent His apostles into the world, that they might teach all nations. It signifies also the coming of the Paraclete into the heart of the Rosy Cross. This is the apex of the mysteries, and there is light in the place of light.

The Ceremony proceeds as in the Winter Solstice, beginning with the speech of the Adeptus Exemptus: *Below is the darkness of material things, etc., and followed by that of the Auxiliary Frater Adeptus, who describes the circle of the place and recites the proper versicles, replacing his light on the altar without extinguishing it and then taking his seat without unclothing. The same procedure is observed by the Second Celebrant; and thereafter the Celebrant-in-Chief rises, with uplifted wand.*

Adeptus Exemptus: The peace of God be with you, O Brethren of the Rosy Cross; and be He realized within you, Who is all days with us, even to the consummation of the world.

He proceeds to the eastern side of the altar, lifts up the light of his office and describes the circle of the place, reciting the proper versicles. Thereafter he replaces his light on the Altar and goes to his invariable seat.

There is the pause of a few moments, and thereafter the Auxiliary Frater Adeptus rises in his place.

Auxiliary Frater Adeptus: The Light of the Lord leadeth us: the Lord is an Everlasting Light: in Thy Light let us see light, shining from the palace at the center, shining from the inmost heart, O King of the greater mysteries. Thy commandment is a lamp; Thy secret law is Light: herein is the light of the eyes. That light shineth in the darkness, and the darkness comprehendeth it not. But as for us we will walk with Thee in the light of the living, the light upon the Israel of the elect, the glory of the Rosy Cross.

The Celebrant-in-Chief and the Second Celebrant have arisen and set open the Door of the Sanctuary. The cross of obligation in the center is under the full light of the Rose.

The High Priest: Frater Lux semper in Coelis (*vel nomen aliud*)**,** on the cross in this sanctuary of the Lord there must be a pledge between us and you, and God shall watch upon the covenant forever.

The Auxiliary Frater Adeptus proceeds to the door of the sanctuary, where he lays aside his wand. He is taken in charge by the High Priest, who leads him within the sanctuary. They turn westward at the cross which is now immediately behind the Auxiliary Frater Adeptus, who extends his arms thereon.

Auxiliary Frater Adeptus: On behalf of you who are my brethren and on my own part, I set myself upon the cross of obligation, to renew my pledges and your own in the presence of the whole Order.

The High Priest binds him to the cross.

The High Priest: May that which we do in your person, collectively and individually, be ratified in Geburah, wherein is the victory of death; be it recorded in Chesed, wherein is the life of resurrection; and the power of the Supernals attest it forever and ever.

The Usher of the Grade gives a battery of one knock and all rise. The High Priest imposes the obligation of the grade. A short pause follows and thereafter:

Auxiliary Frater Adeptus *(while still bound upon the Cross):* May the brethren of this Holy Order be confirmed and strengthened in me; and as I give expression for testimony in the whole personality of Adepti Minores under the obedience of this sacred rite, so may its high end be realized in them and so also in me.

THE HIGH PRIEST: Descend, Auxiliary Frater Adeptus, from the cross of glory in Tiphereth, and the majesty of its light be with you from henceforth and forever.

He unbinds the Third Celebrant and leads him to the door of the sanctuary. As they pause on the threshold:

THE HIGH PRIEST: Fratres et Sorores, in this house of the Holy Spirit, remember that the life of the cross is the way of the mystery of God.

They return to their places, closing but not securing the door of the sanctuary. All the brethren are seated, and there is the pause of a few moments. **THE HIGH PRIEST** *rises and says:* Raise up, we beseech Thee, etc. *The ceremony proceeds to its*

Ceremonies of the Fellowship of the Rosy Cross

conclusion as in The Festival of the Winter Solstice.

The First Order Of The Rosy Cross

World of Action
Part IV

The Ceremony of Consecrating
A Temple for the Mysteries of
The First and Second Orders

The Consecration of a Temple of the Rosy Cross may arise in either of two manners: (i) in response to a petition presented to the Chief of the Rite in the names of at least seven Brethren who are living members of the Fellowship, i.e., are attached to some active Temple or Temples; (2) By the power vested in the Chief of the Rite for the time being, in the exercise of his sole discretion; but he shall be bound on his own part to proceed in conformity with the General Rule of the Fellowship, so that the title of each Temple may be clear and regular.

The petitioners in the one case, and the co-opted brethren in the other, together with the joining members and visitors, being assembled in the vestibule, or in a room adjacent to the place chosen for consecration as a Temple, the Imperator, who has assumed already his vestments and insignia, gives a battery of one knock and makes the first proclamation thus, lifting up his wand of office:

IMPERATOR: Fratres et Sorores in the Fellowship of the Rosy Cross, the Lord is our light and our help. In the Name of Him Who rescues us from the darkness and the unredeemed places, and by the power in me abiding, I call upon you to assume the vesture of your rank and grades. Do Thou clothe us in Thy grace and truth, Great Master of all our ways.

The members put on their clothing and insignia. The Acting Fratres Thurificans et Aquarius assume also their surplices and see that the vessels of their respective offices are prepared and charged with live fire and with water.

When all things are in readiness, a procession is formed with-out, headed by the Imperator of the Rite. He is followed by the Fratres Thurificans et Aquarius, side by side, the Banner-Bearers and the brethren in the order of their grades, two and two in like manner.

When the Chief of the Rite reaches the door of the place about to be consecrated, he comes to a pause thereat, lifts up his wand and says:

IMPERATOR: May this door be blessed, sanctified and commended to the Lord. May it be ever as a gate leading to the Land of the Living for those who enter here by.

The Imperator opens the door and crosses the threshold, saying:

IMPERATOR: Invest our portals, O Lord; consecrate and guard our thresholds; vouchsafe to visit this place.

The procession passes by the north toward the east of the hall, he who has been deputed to act as Ostiarius entering last and securing the door behind him. He remains on the hither side of the door. When the Chief of the Rite has reached the due east he pauses and faces west. The Fratres Thurificans et Aquarius take up their places on either side of him, also facing west. The members of the higher grades pass on to the southern side of the hall and stand by their seats in that quarter. The members of the lower grades halt on the northern side, standing by their seats.

The Imperator of the Rite proceeds to the consecration of Fire and Water in the terms of the First Portal Grade of the Rosy Cross.

The Fratres Thurificans et Aquarius have parted to the right and left as before. The incense is kept fuming. The Imperator lifts up his hands, holding his wand of office.

IMPERATOR: The power of the world is Thine, and Thine is also the glory. Send down Thy power upon me. Make of me a free channel, through which Thy grace shall pass and authorize the solemn consecration that I am about to perform in Thy Name.

The Imperator and his assistants turn eastward. The prayer at the east and assoilment take place as exhibited in the Ritual of the Grade of Neophyte.

[Editor's note: Next two pages were missing from the original document]

IMPERATOR: In the name of the Water of Regeneration and by the Font of Life, flowing from the World of Life, quickening the hearts of men, I purify and dedicate this altar to the service of the Rosy Cross, being part of the Divine service. May those who are pledged hereon enter into the life of purity, and may the power that leads them in the mystical paths of our Fellowship through the worlds of return to God, bring them in due time to that place, beyond this temple, wherein the double cube of the altar unfolds as a cross of Life.

Having returned to the eastern side of the altar, he gives back the vessel and aspergillus, taking the thurible from Frater Thurificans, who receives the wand from Frater Aquarius and retains it. The Imperator offers incense as previously at the four sides of the altar and on the upper surface, saying as he moves through the quarters:

IMPERATOR: By the Fire of salvation, and by the incense that Michael the High Priest offers on the Supernal altar, I consecrate and dedicate this altar to the service of the Rosy Cross, being part of the Divine service. May those who make hereon the offering of their lives in sacrifice be accepted as holy oblations, and when the perishable part of us each has been burnt to ashes, may the soul ascend to GOD — as the sparks fly upward.

The Imperator restores the thurible to Frater Thurificans and moves to the western side of the altar, where he faces east. He lifts up the bread salver and supports it on his left hand.

IMPERATOR: By the power in me vested, and in the name of Melchisedek, priest of the Most High God, I bless ✠, dedicate ✠ and consecrate ✠ this vessel for the food of man. May those who partake herefrom, under the obedience of this Holy Rite, be nourished in a spiritual sense with the bread of Life, the substance of things Divine communicated to the soul of man.

The Imperator lays down the salver and now lifts up the chalice.

IMPERATOR: By the power in me vested, and in the Name of Melchisedek, priest of the Most High God, I bless ✠, dedicate ✠ and consecrate ✠ this vessel for the food of man. May those who partake herefrom, under the obedience of this Holy rite, be nourished in a spiritual sense with the blessed wine of the Kingdom, wine of Divine Life and wine of Union. May they realize in their inmost souls that it is super-essential blood and that this blood is Life.

The Imperator puts down the chalice, opens the lamp and lights it. Having closed it again, he raises the lamp on high.

IMPERATOR: Thou art my lamp, O Lord. The Lord is my light. The Lord shall enlighten my darkness. The torch of a faithful guide goes before me in the dark ways. I shall pass through the paths of darkness. O kindle Thy Light in my heart. By the power in me vested, and in the name of the Great White Light shining from the Great White Throne, I bless ✠, dedicate ✠ and consecrate ✠ this outward and sacramental sign of the light shining from within. May the eyes of its bearer look ever to the perfect day.

The Imperator lays down the lamp. The banners of the temple are brought up. He raises each of them in succession and consecrates them together in the one formula.

IMPERATOR: Thou art our banner, O Lord, and Thy banner is love flowing over us. Lift up our banners of love on the high mountain of our desire for Thee. By the power in me vested, and in the Name of the Omnipotent and Eternal

God, Who is the blessing and consecration of all things, I bless ✠, dedicate ✠ and consecrate ✠ this banner of the Rosy Cross to mark the east of the temple and to point the path upward that leads through the days and the years, even into the mystery of God. I bless ✠, dedicate ✠ and consecrate ✠ this banner of the Rosy Cross to mark the west of the temple, to divide the light from the darkness and to reflect on the outer ways the peace of the ways that are within.

The bearers erect the banners at their proper points in the temple. The Imperator proceeds to consecrate the altar-symbol. He takes the aspergillus from Frater Aquarius, and sprinkles the symbol cross-wise.

IMPERATOR: Blessed be this sacrament of our Fellowship, and blessed be She by whom the waters of our desires are spiritualized.

He returns the aspergillus and takes the thurible from Frater Thurificans. The Imperator censes the symbol.

IMPERATOR: By the power in me vested as Chief of the Rite and keeper of this sacred mystery, I bless ✠, dedicate ✠ and consecrate ✠ this sacrament of our Fellowship with Fire. Blessed be She by whom the will is uplifted in the fire of a sacred purpose that attains its term in God.

He returns the thurible and then exalts the symbol, holding it with both hands.

IMPERATOR: May the Holy Shekinah descend and dwell in this temple, shining as an abiding presence in the centre of this sacred symbol. The rose of the world are Thou, O high lady of quest, leader of the quest in God. From the Center to the four quarters extend the rays of Thine influence. From the four quarters to the Center the grace of Thine attraction draws. Bring us to the rest in the Center, that we may repose under the shadow of Thy wings. Fulfill us in the activity of the Center, the intercourse and joy of union. The Guide of the Paths art Thou, and Thine are the worlds of quest. Lady of severity and judgment on the side of the fear of the Lord, come to us in the fear of separation. Lady of compassion and of mercy on the side of the love of the Lord, come to us in the love of the Holy One. Lady of benediction, Lady of the Middle Pillar and all the kingdom of benignity, lead us from the kingdom of this world, that we may behold the bounty of our Master and the sun of righteousness in Tiphereth. Lead and still lead us onward, and in the World of Supernal Knowledge, show unto us that Jehovah is Elohim in the union of God and His Shekinah.

The Imperator deposits the rose-cross symbol in the middle place of the altar and receives his wand. He passes with the sun to the throne of The Master of the Temple and proceeds to bless and to consecrate with Fire. The Fratres Thurificans et Aquarius have followed him. He receives the thurible in exchange for his Wand.

IMPERATOR: By the power in me vested, and by the grace descending from Chokmah through the pillar and paths of mercy,

I bless ✠, dedicate ✠, and consecrate ✠ with Fire this throne of the Master of the Temple. May the Fire of supernal wisdom flow over the temple and its members. I bless the work of the Master in the name of victory, in the power of the grade of Philosophus, and I hail him by the secret name of FRATER THEOTOKOS, ID EST, A DEO NATUS.

He gives back the thurible in exchange for his wand. He turns now to the west, with wand lifted up.

IMPERATOR: Fratres et Sorores in the Fellowship of the Rosy Cross, I proclaim that the pillar of mercy in the Tree of Life, on the return journey to God, has its basis in this temple and is represented by the throne of the Master, who is a living symbol of the Sephira Netzach.

The Imperator proceeds with the sun to the throne of the Warden of the Temple, followed by the Fratres Thurificans et Aquarius. He proceeds to bless and consecrate with Water receiving the aspergillus from Frater Aquarius in exchange for his wand.

IMPERATOR: By the power in me vested, and by the grace descending from Binah through the pillar and paths of severity, I bless ✠, dedicate ✠ and consecrate ✠ with Water this throne of the Warden of the Temple. May the waters of understanding flow over the temple and its members. I bless the work of the Warden in the name of glory, in the virtue of the grade of Practicus, and I hail him by the Secret Name of FRATER CHRISTOPHOROS, ID EST, CHRISTUM FERENS.

He gives back the aspergillus in exchange for his wand. He turns now to the west with wand lifted up.

IMPERATOR: Fratres et Sorores in the Fellowship of the Rosy Cross, I proclaim that the pillar of justice in the Tree of Life, on the return journey to God, has its basis in this temple and is represented by the throne of the Warden, who is a living symbol of the Sephira Hod.

The Imperator proceeds with the sun to the seat of the Guide in the middle place of the temple, followed by the Fratres Thurificans et Aquarius. He proceeds to bless and consecrate the seat of the Guide with Fire and Water. He takes the aspergillus in exchange for his wand.

IMPERATOR: By the power in me vested, by the union Of mercy and judgment, by the ineffable virtues and graces coming down from the Crown of the Tree, through the pillars and paths of benignity, I bless ✠, dedicate ✠ and consecrate ✠ with Water: *(then returning the aspergillus and taking the thurible)* I bless ✠, dedicate ✠ and consecrate ✠ with Fire the seat of the Guide of this temple. May Divine understanding above all earthly knowledge, the wisdom enthroned in the Highest and the Light of the Father of Mercies meet in the pillar of benignity, flowing over the temple and its members. I bless the work of the Guide in the name of the Holy foundation, the sacrifice of the just therein, and in the mystery of the grade of Theoreticus. I hail him by the secret name of DESMOS MONADOS, ID EST, VINCULUM UNIONIS.

He gives back the thurible, receives and uplifts his wand.

IMPERATOR: Fratres et Sorores in the Fellowship of the Rosy Cross, I proclaim the bond of union, the mystery of espousals in God and the work of the Guide therein, who is a living symbol of the Sephira Yesod.

The Imperator passes directly to the seats in the due west, followed by the Fratres Thurificans et Aquarius. He proceeds to bless and consecrate the seats in the west with Water and with Fire. He takes the aspergillus in exchange for his wand.

IMPERATOR: By the power in me vested, and in the name of Shekinah descending to dwell in the hearts of men, I bless ✠, dedicate ✠ and consecrate ✠ with Water (*then returning the aspergillus and taking the thurible*): ✠ I bless ✠ dedicate ✠ and consecrate ✠ with Fire these seats of the Herald and his ministers. May the graces and powers of all the mystical worlds, emanating one from another and poured upon the kingdom of this world, flow over the temple and its members. I bless the work of the Herald and their work who serve with him as the bearers of Sacramental Water and Fire. I bless them in the name of the Kingdom and in the mystery of the grades of Malkuth.

He gives back the thurible in exchange for his wand. He turns now to the east, with wand lifted up.

IMPERATOR: Fratres et Sorores in the Fellowship of the Rosy Cross, I proclaim that the pillar of benignity in the Tree of

Life, on the return journey to God, has its basis in this temple and is represented by the seat of the Herald, or Proclamator and Lucifer of the Rite, who is a living symbol of the Sephira Malkuth.

The Imperator proceeds to the east, followed by the Fratres Thurificans et Aquarius, who part and go to their seats, which are respectively in the south and north of the temple, at the head of the two columns formed by the unofficial brethren. The Imperator stands between the thrones of the east, facing west.

Imperator: I proclaim that the Salvator Mundi Temple (*vel Templum aliud*) is duly dedicated and consecrated to the Glory of God in the Highest.

The procedure that follows hereon is the appointment and investiture of officers. The brethren of the First and Second Orders are led forth at this point from the temple, and the Master Designate is installed according to the Ritual of the Inner Working. The brethren are recalled and the ceremony proceeds according to the Ritual of the Equinox.

The Master of the Temple proceeds in the next place to open the newly consecrated temple in the grade of Neophyte, the prayer at the east, the assoilment of the temple and the blessing of the Water and Fire being omitted.

In the event of there being a postulant for reception into the Order, the Ceremony of Initiation follows.

The laws of the Fellowship of the Rosy Cross are read in full, as also the authorized by-laws, the latter being put for confirmation by the brethren.

Any general business set forth in the agenda of the consecration summons is then taken.

The temple is closed according to the Ritual of the Grade of Neophyte.

HERE ENDS THE SOLEMN CEREMONY OF CONSECRATING A TEMPLE OF THE ROSY CROSS FOR THE MYSTERIES OF THE FIRST AND SECOND ORDERS.

Ceremonies of the Fellowship of the Rosy Cross

The Third Order Of The Rosy Cross

World of Creation
Part VII

The Ceremony of Consecration for a
Temple of the Third Order

The consecration of a temple for the mysteries of the Third Order, in the grades of adeptship, either presupposes the existence of a lower temple working the rites of the Fellowship in the Worlds of Formation and Action, the Portal of the Third Order included, or such a temple must be opened and consecrated within twelve months thereafter. This law arises from the symbolism of the Tree of Life, the parts and worlds whereof cannot subsist in separation one from another. It is for this reason that the festivals of the Winter and Summer Solstice begin and must always begin with the Pars Magna Secreta, being a derivation from the Portal of the Fourth Order.

The consecration of a new house of the Holy Spirit or temple of the Third Order may come to pass in either of the two ways which warrant the consecration of temples for the mysteries of the First and Second Orders, as specified by the rubrics attached to the ritual provided for that purpose in the World of Action.

The arrangement of the house follows the unwritten precedents. On the day and at the hour appointed, the brethren of all grades in the World of Creation, having assembled and clothed, take their seats in the body of the temple under charge of the Usher of the Rite, who should be preferably an Adeptus Exemptus. The temple is lighted only by two candles on the pillars which stand on either side of the sanctuary door.

The Imperator of the fellowship, or his substitute lawfully appointed, speaks as High Priest of the ceremony from within the most holy sanctuary.

THE HIGH PRIEST: I testify that the Fellowship of the Rosy Cross is perfect in the body of adeptship. May the Divine Spirit therein bear witness from Daath on the threshold of the holy supernals, from henceforth and forever. The witness is also in the world, in the holy houses of the Fellowship. The Lord give increase thereof, and the glory of the Lord visit us. May the great white Light of the Divine Spirit come down.

The Light of the Rose illuminates the Sanctuary suddenly and shines through the walls thereof. The Usher of the Rite rises in his place and turns up the lights of the Temple saying:

THE USHER OF THE RITE: O send out Thy Light and Thy truth. Let them lead us; let them bring us unto Thy holy hill and the everlasting tabernacle of Thy service.

The High Priest opens the door of the sanctuary and is seen by the brethren of all grades in the vestments and insignia of High Priest in the Portal of the Fourth Order. He lifts up his wand of office.

THE HIGH PRIEST: Salvete, Fratres et Sorores, Roseae et Aureae Crucis. The peace of God be with you in the Light of the supernals and the consolation of Christ mystical, the Spirit Who is within.

The Usher of the Rite, rising in his place, gives a battery of one knock and turns westward.

THE USHER OF THE RITE: Vigilate, Fratres et Sorores.

Thereafter he resumes his seat.

THE HIGH PRIEST: Honorable and adept brethren, the counsel is faithful and true that the keepers of a sacred tradition, and of outward signs and symbols of an experience that is within, should maintain and hand on the mysteries, to which end it has been given us at this time to consecrate a house of man as a sanctuary of Divine service and a temple of the Holy Spirit. I pray that herein, as in other holy places and houses of the Rosy Cross, we may hear the voice of our symbolic founder and Loving Father speaking in the symbols of the Word. May the work of the World of Creation be performed in the grace of its sacraments, the work of the Christ Life in the mystery of the Second Birth, the blessed death of the mystic whose eyes are closed in Christ, the union with Christ the Spirit, and the glory of Resurrection in God.

He proceeds to the assoilment of the temple according to the Ritual of the Grade of Neophyte in the Portal of the Rosy Cross, and thereafter returns to his place on the threshold of the sanctuary, where he stands facing the east. The Usher of the Rite gives a battery of one knock and all present rise up. The High Priest has put aside his wand of office and now extends his arms.

THE HIGH PRIEST: Thy Word, O Lord, is imminent in all creation; Thy sanctity finds expression; Thy love manifests therein. May they be declared also in me, working in humility of heart — as a servant of sacred mysteries — the rites of this mystical Order. May Thy blessing, as a water of Life, descend here upon us. May Thy presence be realized in our hearts and within this hidden temple, apart from the world, which we are about to dedicate to Thy service. May the fruits of Thy higher law be administered to the dwellers herein, to those also who shall knock at the door without and unto whom that door shall open. May they attain union with Thee and the peace which we implore at the Center. Amen.

The High Priest faces west and the brethren resume their seats.

The Usher of the Rite passes to the eastern end of the temple on the southern side, over against the sanctuary, where the instruments of consecration are placed on a small table. He brings them in succession to the High Priest, presenting them with both hands, his head being bent reverently. The High Priest consecrates the salt.

THE HIGH PRIEST: Vouchsafe, O Lord, to remember the salt of Thy Covenant, and to bless this creature of salt, that it may be sanctified for the consecration of the temple and holy sanctuary which we are about to dedicate to Thy Service. I bless this salt in Thy name, O Holy God ✠ that for all who seek the mystic way and who serve herein it may be a sign of life and incorruption, the Second Birth and the

Word attained in Thee. May we be salted with the salt of the Kingdom. May wisdom from the seat of Wisdom abide herein. May this salt of the earth become unto us a heavenly salt, a sign of that Divine virtue by which the souls of men are purified.

Thereafter the High Priest consecrates the ashes.

THE HIGH PRIEST: When his earthly part has been burnt to ashes, the spirit of man shall ascend — as the sparks fly upward. Vouchsafe, O Lord, to bless this creature of ash. May it become a fertile earth and bring forth the Tree of Life, to feed the nations. I bless these ashes in Thy name, O Holy God ✠ that they may be sanctified for the consecration of this temple and holy sanctuary that we are about to dedicate to Thy service. May they symbolize a healing medicine, profitable to body and soul for all those who invoke Thy holy name here in.

He mingles a sufficient part of the salt with the ashes.

THE HIGH PRIEST: Salt of Eternal Wisdom ✠, salt of the Second Birth ✠, ash whence the new earth springs ✠, be all things accomplished herein through the grace which comes down from Thee, O Father of Love, and is administered to all things. Amen.

Thereafter the High Priest consecrates the incense.

THE HIGH PRIEST: Master of all our hearts, which burn for Thee, vouchsafe to bless and sanctify this creature of sweet incense which I now consecrate in Thy name ✠, that it may be a sign of aspiration and ascent of the mind to Thee, and that we may call the place holy wherein its smoke ascends.

He has cast incense on the fire in the thurible held up by the Usher of the Rite. Thereafter he consecrates the oil.

THE HIGH PRIEST: It is written: If any man be sick among you, let him call in the priests of the church, and let them pray over him, anointing him with oil in the name of the Lord. And the prayer of faith shall save the sick man; and the Lord shall raise him up; and if he be in sins they shall be forgiven him. Purify this creature of oil, O Lord: sanctify it, Holy Messias: bless it, eternal God. In Thy name, O Lord, I consecrate this creature of oil, that it may heal the sickness of the House and reform its ways in Thee. So shall it signify to us the peace of Thy word, which stills the troubled waters of the soul, the restless sea of our desires, and there follows a great calm.

Thereafter the High Priest consecrates the lamp of the sanctuary, which has been kindled by the Usher of the Rite.

THE HIGH PRIEST: O send out Thy light and Thy truth: may they bring us unto Thy holy hill and to Thy tabernacle. Discover unto us Thy light in the house which we have built for Thy service. Vouchsafe, O Lord, to bless this fire and light, that it may sanctify the place of our mysteries. For the glory of Thy name, O Lord: in the name of our holy religion: by the invisible mountain of wisdom, on which we ascend to Thee: I consecrate ✠ this creature of fire and light as a sign of the holy purpose which forms our wills in Thee, by which we are sealed unto Thee as a people set apart and chosen, and by which — in the power of my office — I seal this house of man, that it may be henceforth and forever a house unto Thee, O God, and a sanctuary of Thy presence.

The Usher of the Rite gives a battery of one knock and all rise. The High Priest resumes his wand and passes with the sun to the entrance door of the temple, which he opens. He stands on one side of it and says:

THE HIGH PRIEST: Let the spirit of the world depart from this place, which is to become a temple of God.

Then, standing in the middle place of the threshold and facing outward, he makes a great cosmic cross ✠ with his wand.

THE HIGH PRIEST: Behold the sign of our attainment. May that which is born of flesh, according to the will of flesh and the lower will of man, keep far henceforth here from. May the Word be made flesh among us, full of grace and truth.

He shuts the door front within, and then facing thereto:

THE HIGH PRIEST: May this door be blessed, sanctified ✠ and commended to the Lord. May it be as a gate opening on Eternal Life to those who enter hereby.

92

And now he faces inward.

THE HIGH PRIEST: Invest our portals, O Lord, and guard our thresholds. Vouchsafe to visit this place.

He passes by north to the portal of holy sanctuary and there puts aside his wand, receiving the vessel of mingled salt and ashes from the hands of the Usher of the Rite. He proceeds to the eastern side of the sanctuary and faces east, scattering the salt and ashes in the form of a cross,

THE HIGH PRIEST: May the part of earth of this temple be purified by the earth of Zion. *(He turns and scatters ashes on the altar in the same manner.)* May this altar of sacrifice be the foundation stone of our election. *(He passes without the sanctuary and scatters ashes in the southern quarter of the temple.)* May the body of this temple be purified by the work of the will in God. *(At the west.)* May it be as the body of God in its manifestation. *(At the north.)* May desire of the house of the Lord purify the body thereof. *(He returns to the door of holy sanctuary and there faces west, lifting up the vessel of ashes.)* May the body of this temple and of all who serve herein be integrated in the mystical body of the Rosy Cross.

The Usher of the Rite receives the vessel of mingled salt and ashes. He places the smoking thurible in the hands of the High Priest, who proceeds to the eastern side of the sanctuary and faces east. He makes the cosmic cross ✠ with the thurible and offers incense thrice.

THE HIGH PRIEST: May the mind of the Father Almighty purify this hidden temple and make a holy sanctuary herein. (*He turns and offers incense over the altar.*) May this altar of sacrifice be purified by the Divine mind. (*He passes without the sanctuary and offers incense in the southern quarter of the temple.*) May the mind of this temple be fashioned in the purpose of God. (*At the west*) May it embody the thought of God. (*At the north.*) May the love of the Father Almighty abide herein. (*He returns to the door of the sanctuary and there faces west, lifting up the thurible.*) May the purified minds of all who serve in this hidden temple be one mind in the Fellowship of the Rosy Cross.

The Usher of the Rite receives the thurible and places the vessel of oil in the hands of the High Priest, who proceeds to the eastern side of the sanctuary and faces east. He pours oil in the form of a cosmic cross.

THE HIGH PRIEST: Purify the house of Thy desire, O Lord, with the gifts and graces of Thy Spirit. (*He turns and pours oil on the altar.*) Purify this altar of sacrifice with the oil of Holy gladness. (*He passes without the sanctuary and pours oil in the southern quarter of the temple.*) Glorify the desires of the house in the work of Thy Holy Will. (*At the west.*) Thy peace is a horn of oil: may peace be unto this temple. (*At the north.*) Purify the heart of this temple; anoint it with Thy holy oil. (*He returns to the door of the sanctuary and there faces west, lifting up the vessel of oil.*) May the heart of this temple be purified in the heart of the Rosy Cross.

The Usher of the Rite receives the vessel of oil and places the lamp of the sanctuary in the hands if the High Priest, who proceeds to the eastern side of the sanctuary and there faces east. He makes the sign of the cosmic cross with the lamp.

THE HIGH PRIEST: May the will of God and of those who are born of God purity this house of dedication. *(He turns and makes the sign of the cosmic cross over the altar.)* And purify this altar, O Lord, to Thy holy purpose. *(He passes without the sanctuary and does likewise in the southern quarter of the temple.)* Send down Thy saving fire: make clean our wills herein. *(At the west.)* Do Thou clothe us with Thy Light as with a garment, and be this temple Thy light embodied. *(At the north.)* Purify it as a heart of light and as a lamp shining in the darkness. *(He returns to the door of the sanctuary and there faces west, lifting up the lamp.)* May the will of this temple, which is the will of Thy serving brothers, be one with Thy holy purpose in the Light of the Rosy Cross.

The Usher of the Rite receives the lamp of the sanctuary and places the vessel of salt in the hands of the High Priest, who proceeds to the eastern side of the sanctuary and there faces east, scattering the salt crosswise.

THE HIGH PRIEST: I have brought a new cruse and have put salt therein, as a symbol of perpetuity and incorruption. I consecrate this temple and Holy Sanctuary in the Name of the Three Supernals. May the presence of Jehovah and Elohim abide herein, for God and His Shekina are One. *(He turns to the altar and scatters salt thereon.)* I consecrate this altar of sacrifice ✠ on the threshold of the holy supernals, in the name of Daath that is the realization of Divine Knowledge. May the Spirit and the bride say, Come — to all those who offer up their life here on. *(He passes without the sanctuary and scatters salt in the southern quarter of the temple.)* I consecrate this temple with salt ✠ invoking the Father in Chokmah. *(At the west.)* I consecrate this temple with salt ✠ invoking the Divine spouse in Tiphereth and the bride in manifestation. *(At the north.)* I consecrate this temple with salt ✠ invoking Taboonah in Binah, the Divine mother of souls. *(He returns to the door of the sanctuary and there faces west, lifting up the vessel of salt.)* I testify to the unity of God and the oneness of the Divine Quest.

The Usher of the Rite receives the vessel of salt and the High Priest resumes his wand.

THE HIGH PRIEST: Fratres et Sorores, holding all grades of the Third Order, as keeper of the sacred mystery under the veils of symbolism and the messenger of Daath, who is servant of the servants of God, I have come down with the highest warrants of the Rosy Cross to integrate a living branch of our Fellowship in the World of Creation, the Christ-Life and the first reflected triad. *(He passes to the throne of the Celebrant-in-Chief, having the white pillar behind it.)* I testify that the pillar of mercy is extended through the World of Mercy to the Supernal Triad in wisdom and that Chesed is the testimony thereof in this holy temple. *(He passes to the throne of the Second Celebrant, having the black pillar behind it.)* I testify that the pillar of severity is extended through the World of Judgment to the Supernal Triad in understanding and that Geburah is the witness thereof in this holy temple. (*He passes to the throne of the Third Celebrant having the cross of obligation behind it.*) I testify that the pillar of benignity is extended through the World of Benignity to the threshold of the supernals in Daath, and that Tiphereth is the testimony thereof in this holy temple.

The High Priest returns to the door of the sanctuary and faces east.

THE HIGH PRIEST: O Thou Who has been our dwelling-place in all generations, for Whose love we have set aside the kingdom of this world, with the spirit and adornment thereof, we have consecrated and set apart to Thy service this place, which henceforth is holy. Place upon it the seal of Thy sanctity, and grant it all heavenly increase. May that which is begun for Thy glory be raised to perfection in Thee. May Thy Presence abide herein, to sanctify our acts and preserve our souls inviolable. May this house of the Holy Spirit, dedicated as a hidden church in the light of the Rosy Cross, be to us now and to many hereafter a gate and threshold of the union.

He turns westward and says:

THE HIGH PRIEST: Fratres et Sorores, the Lord guard our coming in and going out, from henceforth and forever. I testify that this Temple is dedicated and consecrated to the

Glory of God in the Highest.

The Usher of the Rite gives a battery of one knock and says:

The Usher of the Rite: Honorable Fratres et Sorores below the rank of Adeptus Exemptus, come forth and follow me.

He leads them from the temple and returns, if qualified to do so. The Adepti Exempti are seated. The throne of the Third Celebrant is removed, and the cross of obligation is replaced by the cubical altar of the 7=4 grade. The symbols of consecrated personality are laid thereon and also the rose-crucifix. On the altar within the sanctuary are placed a chalice containing sacramental wine, covered by a paten, on which is unleavened bread. A white cloth is folded over these vessels.

The High Priest passes within the sanctuary and performs the sacred ceremonies of the Pars Magna Secreta in the ritual of the winter solstice. In this manner the First Celebrant-in-Chief of the new temple receives his titles and warrants.

The temple is opened in the grade of Adeptus Exemptus by the High Priest himself. The challenging of the faithful witness takes place immediately thereafter, according to the ritual of the winter solstice in Mysterium Chesed. The text is followed throughout and the closing taken. The Adepti Majores are recalled.

The temple is opened in the grade of Adeptus Major by the High Priest. The challenging of the faithful witness takes place immediately thereafter, as in Mysterium Geburah. The text is followed throughout, but the Celebrant Elect resumes his place in the body of the temple. The closing is then taken. The Adepti Minores are recalled.

The temple is opened in the grade of Adeptus Minor by the High Priest. The cubical altar has been removed. The sanctuary altar is now in the center of the temple and the cross of obligation in the sanctuary. Three unlit candles are set upon the altar, in the center of which are the veiled sacramental vessels.

The past celebrants who are the assistants remove their vestments. All unofficial brethren being seated, the High Priest returns to the eastern end of the sanctuary, where he makes the affirmation concerning the faithful priest, as in Mysterium Tiphereth. The answer hereto is given by the Usher of the Rite leading the Celebrant-in-Chief to kneel before the cross of obligation. The text is followed throughout, except that the Celebrant-Elect descends from the cross in sight of the brethren and is at once invested with the robes and insignia by the High Priest, who leads him outside the sanctuary, kindles his candle on the altar and places it in his hands. The High Priest takes his seat.

The Celebrant-in-Chief circumambulates the temple with the proper versicles. After their investiture the Second and Third Celebrants circumambulate the temple reciting the versicles allotted to each, as in Mysterium Tiphereth. The cross of obligation is removed and the altar replaced in the sanctuary. The final proclamation of the Celebrant-in-Chief is omitted, and the closing is taken in the grade of Adeptus Minor.

Here ends the Solemn Ceremony of Consecrating a Temple of the Rosy Cross for the Mysteries of the Third Order.

The Fourth Order Of The Rosy Cross

World of the Supernals
Part II

The Ceremony of Enthroning a
Keeper of the Sacred Mystery

The temple is prepared for the mysteries of the portal of Daath, with the variations that here follow. The banners of the paths leading to all grades are congregated at their proper symbolical points. The several altar banners are grouped in correspondence with the Sephiroth to which the paths lead up, as arranged in the Tree of Life, and so also are the banners of the holy sanctuary in the grade of Adeptus Minor. The door of the sanctuary is open to its full extent, and the altar of the portal of Daath has the sacred vessels and the lighted candles thereon. The pillars are at a short distance in front of the sanctuary, with the banners of the Rosy Cross corresponding hereunto. The vestments and insignia of a High Priest lie folded on a cushion of red silk, and this is placed on a table, where there is also a salver containing red, white and blush roses. The table is at a convenient point in proximity to the door of holy sanctuary — as, for example, on the southern side of the pillar of mercy. There is full light everywhere.

The Imperator Elect is kneeling at the western side of the altar, with arms clasped thereon and with bowed head. There is a palm branch laid across his hands. The brethren of the Third Portal Grade are seated, clothed and in silence, in the body general of the temple. The seat of the Officiating Epopt is in front of the brethren, all facing east.

The Officiating Epopt gives a battery of one knock using the wand that he carries.

It is that of an Usher of the Rite in all grades of the Fellow-ship, and is therefore surmounted with a dove of peace. He raises his wand and proceeds to

The Solemn Ceremony of Opening The Holy Temple

The Officiating Epopt: Fratres et Sorores, the peace of the Eternal be upon you in the heart of eternal peace. And peace, be still, my brethren. Silence is in the Mouth of the Almighty One. The Word is known in the heart, when the heart is Love.

He pauses and lowers his wand. Thereafter, again he raises it.

The Officiating Epopt: I testify from the seat of experi-ence that God is all in all.

He pauses and lowers his wand. He lifts up his face and wand. All rise.

The Officiating Epopt: Assist me to open, O Lord, this consecrated temple and house of the Holy Spirit in the grade which is above all grades, in the perfect mystery of union.

And then with bowed head,

THE OFFICIATING EPOPT: By the power which is grace of that mystery, I open the portal of Daath, as a door in the house of Thy knowledge. Behold, Thou art with me all days, to the consummation of our being at the Center.

He bends his right knee, and so also the brethren.

THE OFFICIATING EPOPT: God opens His temple, my brethren — the place of His union.

He passes eastward and stands between the pillars, facing west.

THE OFFICIATING EPOPT: Fratres et Sorores, assist me to open this temple for the high office of enthronement. He gives unto His people a leader. The Lord shall keep His treasure and the tabernacle of His holy mystery. He shall raise up a shepherd in the land and set up a ruler over us, in the name of His covenant. Thou shall guide us therefore, our Master, and our choice shall be made in Thee.

He gives a battery of one knock.

THE OFFICIATING EPOPT: Fratres et Sorores, I declare this temple open for the work which is put into our hands, and a Keeper of our sacred mystery shall be enthroned herein.

THE HIGH OFFICE OF ENTHRONEMENT

The unofficial brethren are seated. The Officiating Epopt proceeds to state the circumstances of that special event which has called the adepti together. When the throne of the headship is vacant owing to the death of an Imperator, he continues as here follows:

THE OFFICIATING EPOPT: Honorable Fratres et Sorores, seeing that we come forth from the Center and that the Center calls us back, I testify that it has pleased our most high father and God, on Whom we depend in all things, and unto Whom in all things we defer, to set free in holiness, from the sacred veils and bonds of his earthly body, the soul of our Most Honoured Frater Electus ex Millibus *(vel nomen aliud)*, KEEPER OF OUR SACRED MYSTERY AND IMPERATOR IN ORDINE ROSEÆ ET AUREÆ CRUCIS.

When the throne of the headship is vacant owing to unavoidable resignation or other circumstances recognized and provided for in the higher constitution of the Fellowship, the Officiating Epopt proceeds thus:

THE OFFICIATING EPOPT: Honorable Fratres et Sorores, I certify that our Most Honored Frater Electus ex Millibus *(vel nomen aliud)*, KEEPER OF OUR SACRED MYSTERY AND IMPERATOR IN ORDINE ROSEÆ ET AUREÆ CRUCIS, has placed his resignation in the hands of the Council of Epopts in the holy house of resurrection *(state here such circumstances as appertain to the case and occasion)*, and the same has been

105

by them accepted in sorrow and fraternity, all ties and bonds of fellowship subsisting as heretofore between him and us.

He proceeds thereafter as follows, in either case.

THE OFFICIATING EPOPT: I testify that the headship has become and is hereby declared vacant. I bear witness also that during the intervening period the council of the Order has assumed the reins of government, in accordance with the laws of the Order, and that there has been no break or intermission in the holy rule of the rite. Moreover, in the exercise of powers thereunto committed, and with the concurrence of him who preceded *(vel affirmatio alia),* I declare that the Honorable Frater Quoniam Tu solus sanctus *(vel nomen aliud)* has been elected and appointed duly as a lawful successor, subject to his plenary profession, his acceptance of the terms of obligation which shall be administered hereinafter and his enthronement in solemn form.

There is *here the pause of a moment.*

THE OFFICIATING EPOPT: May God be therefore with us. May His Divine Presence be declared in this holy temple, to ratify and confirm our acts. May the Light of His unity be reflected upon the unity of our Order and abide as grace in its headship, that these may be one in their purpose, one in working and one in aspiration toward the term. So shall this Fellowship of the Rosy Cross hold its warrants from many spheres, many worlds of initiation, worlds of sacred mystery, worlds of attainment.

The Officiating Epopt resumes his proper seat. While still standing hereat and now facing East:

THE OFFICIATING EPOPT: I call upon the Honorable Frater Quoniam Tu solus sanctus *(vel nomen aliud),* successor elect to the vacant throne of the headship, to testify in this house of ascension concerning the peace of its sanctuary and all the holy houses of the Rosy Cross.

The Imperator Elect rises from his knees, comes forward and stands between the pillars in his white robe and girdle, but wearing no insignia, save only the palm branch, which he carries in his right hand. The Officiating Epopt is seated.

THE OFFICIATING EPOPT *(with the other Brethren in unity):* O quantum magnale pacis.

A pause follows, during which the Imperator Elect remains in his place between the pillars.

THE OFFICIATING EPOPT: Ave, Frater Quoniam Tu solus sanctus *(vel nomen aliud).* The Council of the Rosy Cross, convened in their holy house of resurrection, according to the laws of the Order, has already issued its decree, and your concurrence has been signified therein. But in the presence of the brethren who are here and now assembled as representatives of the whole Fellowship, I demand whether you are free, able and willing to take into your heart and discharge the sacred duties of the headship, and to enter into those solemn bonds of service which are imposed on an Imperator of the Rite.

THE IMPERATOR ELECT: In the Name of God, Who is my end: so help me God.

The Officiating Epopt gives a battery of one knock and all rise.

THE OFFICIATING EPOPT: Let the Light of the Divine leading be called down upon the counsels of our prudence.

THE PRAYER BEFORE ENTHRONEMENT

THE OFFICIATING EPOPT: Giver of understanding and of peace in the days of life, Giver of the union which is realized in the peace of stillness, Giver of the knowledge in experience which is wisdom attained in Thee: bestow on us understanding in choice, grace in the fruition thereof, wisdom to know Thy will and strength to do it with our might. We have chosen this man and our brother, amidst prayers for Thy guidance, to rule over the holy houses which are dedicated to Thy service. Ratify the choice which we have made. Grant that he may increase in us and that we may be enlarged in him by all graces which come from Thee. Bless him in all his ways and bless us richly in the gifts and zeal of him. May we work together in unity, reflecting here below the eternal unity of Thy being. Grant in fine that — proceeding with him and in him — we may enter into Thy deeper knowledge, and that our wings of desire may bear forward our beloved brethren, through all the paths and grades, seeking the crown of the kingdom, to abide in Thy love for ever.   Amen.

The Imperator Elect has prayed eastward, with bowed head and hands crossed over the palm branch. He turns westward. The Officiating Epopt and brethren return to their seats. There is silence for a space, and thereafter:

THE SEARCHING OF THE IMPERATOR ELECT

THE OFFICIATING EPOPT: Do you promise to preserve in your heart and translate into your life and actions the Divine symbolism of this house of ascension in God?

THE IMPERATOR ELECT: In the name of God, Who is my end: so help me God.

THE OFFICIATING EPOPT: Do you promise, ever and continually, in all your works and ways, to seek and — God aiding — to attain a deeper knowledge of the union through Christ in God?

THE IMPERATOR ELECT: In the name of God, Who is my end: so help me God.

THE OFFICIATING EPOPT: Do you promise in the consecration of the mystical bread and wine — which it will be your part henceforth to perform in the sanctuary of this house of ascension—that you will proceed invariably in conscious and willing concurrence with the highest intention of the mystery, and that to the fullest extent of your power you will place upon the clean oblation the signature of your realization in God?

THE IMPERATOR ELECT: In the name of God, Who is my end: so help me God.

THE OFFICIATING EPOPT: Do you promise to be about the business of this holy house and the other houses and temples, leaving unto the perishable word and the custodians thereof those things that pass with the world, in so far as human weakness may consent hereto?

THE IMPERATOR ELECT: In the name of God, Who is my end: so help me God.

THE OFFICIATING EPOPT: Do you promise to instruct the sons and daughters of our Fellowship, by word and example, with all your heart and will, so far as in you lies, in the high inward truths and mystic ends of the Order?

THE IMPERATOR ELECT: In the name of God, Who is my end: so help me God.

THE OFFICIATING EPOPT: Do you promise to maintain the meekness which consents to dignity and all high patience becoming to a spiritual ruler?

THE IMPERATOR ELECT: In the name of God, Who is my end: so help me God.

THE OFFICIATING EPOPT: Do you promise to preserve in faith and transmit intact to your successor the mystery of the Rosy Cross according to our exalted construction, and that you will neither alter nor vary the symbols of that mystery, nor the essential words thereof?

THE IMPERATOR ELECT: In the name of God, Who is my end: so help me God.

THE OFFICIATING EPOPT: All these things, and all other good things, may the Lord grant unto thee, and preserve and strengthen thee in every goodness.

The Officiating Epopt gives a battery of one knock, and all rise.

THE OFFICIATING EPOPT: Honorable Frater and Successor Elect to the headship, I call upon you now to repeat your Sacramental Name and to say after me

THE OBLIGATION OF AN IMPERATOR ELECT

I, Frater Quoniam Tu solus sanctus (*vel nomen aliud*), being an Adeptus Exaltatus, testifying in the house of ascension to the glory of the Rosy Cross and the ineffable life of experience behind the veils of symbolism, do hereby and herein, in the freedom of the will in union and with purpose realized in God, swear fidelity to my higher soul and to the spirit which is Christ therein. I will walk in the way of the Spirit and will abide in fellowship with the Hidden Master of the Rosy Cross, acting as His vicegerent and spokesman in all the temples of this holy and sovereign Order, which is here committed to my hands. In assuming the throne of the headship I will hold myself henceforward as servant-in-chief of my brethren, who are servants and handmaidens of God. In the place of authority I will work only for the spiritual profit and perfection of those who are placed in my charge, in my own and in their person maintaining the rule of the Order, for the extension and diffusion of that knowledge which is found within, for the love of our Hidden Master and the Divine, All-Holy ends. May the Spirit and the bride bear witness and God Who is all in all.

Whosoever as acted as Minister in Service of the temple for the preparation of all therein, having retired behind the sanctuary or otherwhere, has kindled and blessed incense and now comes forward, bearing the thurible, which he places in the hands of the Officiating Epopt, receiving and putting aside his wand.

The Officiating Epopt draws toward the new Imperator and offers incense before him.

The Officiating Epopt (at the first censing): May that which in thee is below be assumed by that which is above. *(At the second censing.)* There are three that rule in thy temple: the will, desire, and mind — let these three be one for the good of our Fellowship. *(At the third censing.)* May the Word be thine and power to manifest the light thereof. *(At the fourth censing.)* Within and without thee, in all thy thoughts and acts, do thou remember the union. *(At the fifth censing.)* The Lord search Thee with the Fire of His Holy Spirit in the heart and in the reins.

The Officiating Epopt falls back slowly, still facing east, and standing before his own seat, he raises the thurible.

The Officiating Epopt: Honorable Frater Quoniam Tu solus sanctus (*vel nomen aliud*), the Lord give unto thee according to thy works.

The Minister in Service receives the thurible. The new Imperator and Officiating Epopt approach one another, pausing in the middle way. The Imperator lays the palm branch in the hands of the Officiating Epopt and says:

Imperator Novus: The Lord give you peace in my days.

He falls back slowly between the pillars, still facing west. The Officiating Epopt comes forward, and having laid the palm branch aside he clothes the new Imperator in the vestments of his office.

The Officiating Epopt (in putting the white cope about him): The Spirit within thee is Christ, the spouse of the soul. I clothe thee as with the vesture of the Spirit, which is the soul restored in purity. Be thine the righteousness of saints. *(In placing the miter on his head.)* Be thy mind an open channel to receive the Divine Influx. *(In fastening on his bosom the red, white and intincted roses.)* May severity and mercy dwell together in unity, meeting in the benignity of thy rule, and may the tree of knowledge become the Tree of Life in the Fellowship of the Rosy Cross. *(Then placing the wand in his hand.)* Rule, therefore, O Master, and be this the sign of Thy power, for this is the Tree of Life.

He draws the new Imperator a short distance in front of the pillars, between which the Minister in Service now places the throne.

THE OFFICIATING EPOPT: We who have elected and appointed, by the power vested in our office, do now install and enthrone thee.

The new Imperator is placed on the throne. The Officiating Epopt turns west, and, having received his wand, gives a battery of one knock.

THE OFFICIATING EPOPT: Fratres et Sorores, my peers and co-heirs in the house of ascension that is in God, I proclaim that Frater Quoniain Tu solus sanctus *(vel nomen aliud)*, having been regularly elected and appointed, rigorously searched and sifted, faithfully professed and pledged, and in fine invested and enthroned, has become hereby and herein Most Honored Imperator of the Fellowship of the Rosy Cross and keeper of its sacred mystery. Now, therefore, as your vicegerent and spokesman, I pledge to him, in all high faith and truth, our reasonable and loving obedience over all that concerns the Order.

He returns to his seat, and still standing thereat, he recites or chants the Triple Benediction, followed by all the brethren.

114

THE OFFICIATING EPOPT: (1) That Thou wouldst vouchsafe to bless this present elected Chief, Master of all, we pray Thee; (2) That Thou wouldst vouchsafe to bless and to sanctify this present elected Chief, Master of all, we pray Thee; (3) That Thou wouldst vouchsafe to bless, sanctify and approve this present elected Chief, duly pledged and enthroned, Master of all, we pray Thee.

The Imperator rises with uplifted wand.

THE IMPERATOR: May the Fellowship of the Rosy Cross testify henceforth and forever, amidst the things which are below, to the eternal things which are above, that the powers of the height may prevail also in the depth and that God may rule His people.

And then, after a short pause:

THE IMPERATOR: Honorable Fratres et Sorores, the purpose of the present convocation having been accomplished in God, for the furtherance of His Divine Ends, I close here and now this holy Office of Enthronement.

The throne is set aside. The Imperator enters the sanctuary as High Priest and celebrates The Mass of Union. When the Closing has been taken, the Officiating Epopt rises in his place and says:

THE OFFICIATING EPOPT: Let us descend by the path of Cheth, even unto Tiphereth.

A procession is formed and the brethren pass into the vestibule, with the Officiating Epopt and Minister of Service carrying the banners of the Rosy Cross before the Imperator, who goes forth last of all.

Here ends the Ceremony of Enthroning a Keeper of the Sacred Mystery in the House of Ascension.

THE PROCLAMATION OF A KEEPER OF THE SACRED MYSTERY IN THE GRADE OF TIPHERETH

The arrangement of house and sanctuary follows the unwritten precedents. The brethren of all grades in the World of Creation are seated, clothed and in silence. The door of the temple opens and the Celebrant-in-Chief enters, followed by the Adeptus Major and Auxiliary Frater Adeptus, walking in single file. Behind them come two Ministers, walking together, bearing the banners of the Rosy Cross, and thereafter the Usher of the Rite, with the banner of the path of Cheth. The New Imperator follows last of all, and the door is closed behind them. They proceed to the east, the Celebrants assuming their invariable stations, and the Imperator passing to his throne on the southern side. The banner of the path of Cheth is placed behind the throne and the banners of the Rosy Cross, respectively east and west beside it. All present have risen to receive the procession and all again are seated, after the Imperator takes his place on the throne.

The temple is opened in the grade of Adeptus Minor, and in the case of the former Imperator having been called from the life of earth, the Commemoration of his Passing takes place in solemn form.

The Celebrant-in-Chief gives a battery of one knock.

ADEPTUS EXEMPTUS: Honorable Fratres et Sorores, seeing that we come forth from the Center and that the Center draws us back, I testify that it has pleased our Most High Father and God, on Whom we depend in all things, and unto Whom in all things we defer, to set free in holiness, from the sacred veils and bonds of his earthly body, the soul of our Most Honoured Frater Electus ex Millibus *(vel nomen aliud)*, KEEPER OF OUR SACRED MYSTERY AND IMPERATOR IN ORDINE ROSEÆ ET AUREÆ CRUCIS.

He turns to the east, with all present.

ADEPTUS EXEMPTUS: We who are stewards of Thy mysteries, O Master of all things; we who are wardens of the gates which lead in fine to Thee; we who have borne Thy charges in common with our Most Honoured Frater Electus ex Millibus *(vel nomen aliud),* thus called from among us, do here and now at Thy bidding relinquish the fellowship that we had in him, with resignation and holy joy. Into Thy loving care we commend his soul, O Lord of all tender compassion, Spirit and spouse of souls. Amen.

117

THE IMPERATOR: Ratify, we beseech Thee, in the life of the world to come, all that he knew of Thy union in the life of earth.

ADEPTUS EXEMPTUS: May the shadowed lights of our symbolism dissolve for him in the glorious realities of being whereof they are the veil and the presage.

THE IMPERATOR: May this be the day of his espousals.

ADEPTUS EXEMPTUS: May he rise into the life which is in Thee, and this is the life of Thy love, the union of the lover and Beloved, world without end.

THE IMPERATOR: World without end art Thou, and this is the life of Thy love, O Love which art Life forever.

ADEPTUS EXEMPTUS: When the Spirit and the soul are one, O Heart of the heart of man.

THE IMPERATOR: May that which is Thine in Thee to That Which is Thee and Thine, to the Father of all, ascend.

ADEPTUS EXEMPTUS: The Oneness of all Oneness.

THE IMPERATOR: The Life of All in all.

ADEPTUS EXEMPTUS: When he who was our brother has attained all things in Thee, O God, grant that we may be drawn after Him.

THE IMPERATOR: Give us peace in our earthly day, as the shadow of that day which is eternal.

ADEPTUS EXEMPTUS: A quiet night after and a perfect end.

All are seated and there is silence for a certain space.* The Celebrant-in-Chief rises.

* NOTE: *When the throne of the headship has become vacant owing to unavoidable resignation, or other circumstances recognized and provided for in the higher constitution of the Fellowship, the Celebrant-in-Chief, after opening in the 5-6 grade, proceeds at once as follows:*

ADEPTUS EXEMPTUS: Honorable Fratres et Sorores, I testify that the Most Honored *F*rater Electus ex Millibus (*vel nomem aliud)*, KEEPER OF OUR SACRED MYSTERY AND IMPERATOR IN ORDINE ROSÆ ET AUREÆ CRUCIS, has placed his resignation in the hands of the house of resurrection (*state here such circumstances as appertain to the case and occasion),* and the same has been by them accepted in sorrow and fraternity, all ties and bonds of fellowship subsisting as heretofore between him and us.

The procedure continues as shown in the text above after the Office of Commemoration.

ADEPTUS EXEMPTUS: Honorable Fratres et Sorores, I testify that Frater Quoniam Tu solus sanctus (*vel nomen aliud)* has been regularly elected and appointed, duly installed and enthroned, and I proclaim him hereby and herein MOST HONORED IMPERATOR OF THE FELLOWSHIP OF THE ROSY CROSS AND KEEPER OF ITS SACRED MYSTERY.

He resumes his seat. The Imperator rises in his turn and recites his profession in the terms appointed for that purpose according to the Ritual of Enthronement. Thereafter he resumes his seat, and the Celebrant-in-Chief rises.

ADEPTUS EXEMPTUS: In the name of the house of resurrection, on my own part and on the part of the Adepti Exempti, as their vicegerent and spokesman, I pledge to the Most Honored Imperator our reasonable and loving obedience in all that concerns the Order.

Thereafter he resumes his seat, and the Second Celebrant rises.

Adeptus Major: In the name of the halls of silence, on my own part and on the part of the Adepti Majores, as their vicegerent and spokesman, I pledge to the Most Honored Imperator our reasonable and loving obedience in all that concerns the Order.

Thereafter he resumes his seat, and the Third Celebrant rises.

Auxiliary Frater Adeptus: By the crucified life of Tiphereth, on my own part and on the part of the Adepti Minores, as their vicegerent and spokesman, I pledge to the Most Honored Imperator our reasonable and loving obedience in all that concerns the Order.

Thereafter he resumes his seat. The Imperator rises and advancing to a middle place in the temple, he lifts up his wand.

THE IMPERATOR: Honorable Fratres et Sorores, the Lord give you peace in my days.

He resumes his seat. The temple is closed in the grade of Adeptus Minor. Thereafter the Celebrant-in-Chief says:

ADEPTUS EXEMPTUS: Let us descend by the path of Ayin, even unto Yesod.

A procession is formed as in the opening ceremony, and the brethren leave the temple.

Here ends the Proclamation of a Keeper of the Sacred Mystery in the grade of Tiphereth.

THE PROCLAMATION OF KEEPER OF THE SACRED MYSTERY IN THE GRADE OF THEORETICUS AND IN THE FIRST PORTAL GRADE OF THE ROSY CROSS

The Temple should be opened in these grades on the day of enthronement, and in whatsoever place the convocations of the lower orders are held. The ceremonial summons to assume the habit, vestments and insignia of the Fellowship is given by the Master of the Temple, who recites also the prayer between the thrones, prior to opening in the grade of Theoreticus. It is thereafter only that the new Imperator enters his temple, preceded by standard bearers, carrying the banners of the Rosy Cross, and by the Thurificans et Aquarius scattering blessed incense and holy water. He proceeds to his throne in the east.

The temple being opened in the grade of Theoreticus, the Master of the Temple announces the resignation or decease of the former Imperator in the terms of the grade of Tiphereth, but there is no further commemoration in the latter case.

The Master of the Temple proclaims the new Imperator, who recites his profession, in the appointed terms.

The pledge of obedience is pronounced by the Master of the Temple on behalf of the grade of Philosophus, by the Warden of the Temple on behalf of the grade of Practicus, and by the Guide of the Path on behalf of the grade of Theoreticus, using the following formula:

122

In the name of our consecrated personality, looking toward the life of rebirth and the mystery of the will in union (or of love in transmutation, or the Light of the mind in God), on my own part and on the part of the Philosophical Brethren (or Practical, or Theoretical) I pledge to the Most Honored Imperator our reasonable and loving service in all that concerns the Order.

(The prayer of peace is recited by the Imperator, and the temple is closed in the grade of Theoreticus.)

THE MASTER OF THE TEMPLE: Let us descend by the Path of Tau, even unto Malkuth.

The temple is opened at once in the grade of Neophyte, and the same procedure follows, but the new Imperator is proclaimed by the Auxiliary Frater Zelator, standing in his proper place with his ministers.

The Imperator communicates the mystical Elements to brethren of all grades, remaining throughout the observance at the eastern side of the altar, facing west. The brethren come round successively, bearing the lamp, and he receives it from each in turn, till his place is taken by the Auxiliary Frater Zelator.

The closing is taken in the grade of Neophyte. The Imperator is conducted from the temple, the Auxiliary Frater Zelator leading the way with lamp and wand, his officers following, scattering blessed incense and Holy Water. The Guide of the

Paths follows, proceeding alone, then the Master and Warden, side by side, the standard bearers, carrying the banners of the Rosy Cross, and the Imperator last of all.

Here ends the Solemn Ceremony of Proclaiming a Keeper of the Sacred Mystery in the Grades below the Portal of the Third Order.

The Ceremony Of Consecration
On The Threshold Of Sacred Mystery
For The Watchers of the Holy House

To the Glory of Thy Name, O Lord, and
the inviolate splendor of the Rosy Cross,
through Christ our Lord within.

✠ Issued for the use of Serving Brothers and Companions of the Order by

the Keeper of the Sacred Rites ✠

✠ Datum in Monte Sancto, ubi aedificatum est Templum Domini ✠

The Master of the Rite, officiating as High Priest, is seated on his throne in the east between the pillars of the temple. He wears a white robe, having a red cross emblazoned thereon and extended from neck to hem. This vestment reaches below the knees, and beneath it is a white alb. He carries a wand surmounted by a Rosy Cross. All present in the sanctuary are clothed in the same manner, the High Priest only wearing an additional white sacerdotal cloak or cope of thin texture. The Priestess, whose wand is crowned with lilies, and her two assistants — these bearing rose-wands — are on the southern side. Other Spokesmen of the Rite are placed in the north. Those who belong to the sanctuary but are taking no active part may be seated on benches facing west and situated north and south of the great altar, which is at a certain distance forward and is served by a Thurificans, installed at either horn. The Symbolum Magnum of the Rose-Cross is erected upon the altar, with flowers and lights about it, in groups of seven and twelve. At the foot of the Cross are four cubes of white alabaster, crystal or white wood, bearing inscriptions. The Ushers of the Rite are placed at the far west of the temple on the southern side, the Watcher of the Sacred Portal and the Herald of the Temple being similarly stationed on the northern side, all facing east. They wear the general black habit of Companions of the Rosy Cross and the distinctive Lamina of their office, which is a cross of Malta shape, decorated by a rose of five petals. The seats of the holy congregation are ranged from east to west, leaving a free space about the walls for circumambulation in the path of the sun. N.B. The Ushers bear respectively roses and lilies as additional jewels on their breasts. There are branches of palms in their hands. Those who abide in the sanctuary have the same mystical flowers in combination, and the inscription about them is: EGO SUM FLOS CAMPI ET LILIUM CONVALLIUM. *Unofficial members of the Holy Congregation have a Calvary Cross of red enamel, depending from a white collar placed about the neck. The High Priest and the Priestess, the other Spokesmen of the Rite, and* [text unintelligible in mss] *sanctuary and passing with the Sun to their appointed places. They take their seals in silence and all lights are extinguished. When the temple is in uttermost darkness, when there is no suggestion of light anywhere, the precincts included, the holy congregation enters, led by the Herald of the Rite, who carries a shrouded lantern. He returns in silence as he came, securing the door behind him and taking up his place thereat. There is now unbroken stillness within, and when this has endured for a brief period, he proceeds to the vestibule, where he salutes the Postulant of the day, saying:*

HERALD: I have followed a certain star through the days and the years, a star that is faithful and true, a star with the voice of hope. I know thereby that all that lives and breathes shall come at length into its own. Be welcome, in the name of the Order, the Grace within the Order and the Inward Fount of Grace.

The Postulant is clothed in the weeds of a pilgrim, or in such other vesture as may be determined from time to time. A cross of rough wood is suspended about his neck, signifying his own manifest existence and all that he carries therein. It is understood that he has been prepared zealously; he has signed the form of profession. It is known that he has a certain disposition towards the inward life and the realization of Christ in His Kingdom, regarded as [text unintelligible in mss] *living; make us Thy robe of glory.*

The Postulant is given also a wallet, in which are blocks of wood variously colored and inscribed. They are significant of the parts of his personality in their normal mode of being. N.B. The outlines of a temple are depicted on one side of the wallet and on the other is an open eye.

HERALD: Dead branches, barren tares: give unto us harvest sheaves. Uplift us into holy sanctuaries: graft us as golden boughs on the Tree of Life.

The Postulant is led slowly and reverently towards the door of the temple and in the course of this progress:

HERALD: There is a knocking at all our doors, and may we be ready to open.

At a short distance from the door itself:

HERALD: Of knocking and opening in temples, remember here and now: think in the heart thereon, because of their meaning. Think of the sacred admissions and of all that follows in advancements. The court of the temple is not without its Neophytes, Watchers and Serving Brothers: the Holy of Holies is not without its priesthood, which ministers and worships there.

The Postulant has been reminded of the Second Birth and its doctrine of high experience in a conference prior to reception.

As they stand on the very threshold:

HERALD: The house awaits thee: Be thou born therein.

Meanwhile, the silence within has been followed by organ music and thereafter by the voice of the High Priest.

THE HIGH PRIEST: The temple is opened in darkness, looking through the dark of dark to light of light beyond and the glory of the Rosy Cross.

The sanctuary is filled for a few moments with the radiance of the great symbol, and again the dark prevails.

THE HIGH PRIEST: Fratres et Sorores, Watchers of our Holy House, amidst the hallows of mystic darkness, I open the work on the threshold of sacred mystery and bear my faithful witness to the cross of Christ.

THE PRIESTESS OF THE RITE: I bear my witness to the Holy Rose, an image of the Lord of glory.

THE HIGH PRIEST: O sacred night of contemplation, vision of the soul therein, and world of union beyond the world of vision. Still we our senses: listen in the soul alone. A Voice shall speak within. Still we the soul itself. Then it is the Voice only, as if to our deepest self there spoke a self beyond.

A battery of one knock and no other is sounded softly on the door by the Herald of the Rite. It is opened by the Watcher from within, and he asks the question of the time, as he stands unseen in the darkness.

WATCHER: Whom have you there?

HERALD: An earthly body which veils the spiritual man and a blessed place of the Presence.

WATCHER: What do you seek at our hands ?

HERALD: I ask you to sanctify the body, that we may look upon that great light which shines from the soul within.

WATCHER: What manner of light, my brother ?

HERALD: Rewarding light of God in those who seek Him out.

WATCHER: What is the end in view?

HERALD: That soul transformed in God through flesh made pure, and justified by holy temple rites, may bear its faithful witness in the world.

The voice of the High Priest intervenes far away in the east.

THE HIGH PRIEST: Lead on this child of man: the darkness seeks the light.

When the door is closed behind them, and while they pause on the inner side:

THE HIGH PRIEST: They know not whither they are going in the ways without; but thou shall learn in the sanctuary of this holy temple.

The Herald conducts the Postulant to a vacant seat set apart for him in the mid-west and thereafter passes to his own place. There is again unbroken stillness in the dark of dark. It is followed by a breathing of slow music, which rises by degrees to a very torrent of sound. A voice breaks in suddenly on the crest of the music. It chants clearly and sweetly

THE HYMN OF THE SOUL IN UNION

I. The Peace of God is the Union: the Union is God with us.

II. There is no life but life, and that is Thou.

III. Thine is the essence and Thine the growth therefrom.

IV. The mercy of Thy Covenant is poured upon those who love Thee.

V. In Thee and Thine Union we become ourselves the Covenant.

VI. Make of us Thine in the Keeping, till Thine is also Thou.

VII. Unity of all the Unity and Oneness found within.

The silence which follows is of certain moments only, and then another voice ordains the mode of contemplation on the blessed path of union, giving intimations concerning it for the leading of inward thought.

THE HIGH PRIEST *(vel alius):* When veils are on me and the clouds about me; when the world clamors and its spirit draws me forth: then art Thou far away. I do not feel Thee, and I see Thee not; I do not know Thee, whether without or within. I am nothing and have nothing: my food is husks. The darkest state of all is when the broken shells seem meat from the King's table. ✠ O cities in the wastes of time, where is the City of God? ✠ But if I abide in the hiddenness, if I keep my soul in silence, if I put away all the presences and forget the forms of thought: then am I aware of Thee. I hear Thee in the still small voice, who have lost Thee amidst the thunders, in all this storm of words. ✠ Where the dark clouds hang out and the fire flashes, Thou and the soul are lost. ✠

The soul is high remembrance, remote and vast and vague; but it is expectation also. ✠ In the great old duration, beyond the modes of change, my deeps were Thine: I look to find Thee there, far past all life of sense. ✠ But here in the house of my exile, here in the bonds of flesh, how did I know of Thee, Master, or come to remember Thee? How did I hear Thee first? As a child at the mother's knee? As a youth in the classes? It is very well. ✠ In the Church, woe is me? What rites, what words of the preacher? Were they not good and true? ✠ What ways of missing the message! I heard of Thee only without who know Thee only within, in the one place of knowledge. ✠ The awareness becomes the presence, and Thou art That. ✠ Where shines Thy light? Where, Master, but within? Not from without or any other-where: O Thou of all things inward, far past the personal self. ✠ Thou the beginning and Thou the end, through and beyond the ages. ✠ Let us contemplate in the heart, my brethren, when the heart is still, when the pulse of outward life is heard no more and time suspends its beatings.

There is a long pause of silence, which grows in tenseness to a vibrant point, and then another voice is raised: it bears true witness on the Rosy Cross.

THE PRIESTESS OF THE RITE *(vel alia):* On sacred temples of the threshold; the promise of peace in temples; odors about the temples; words of sacred odors and tongues of incense; houses of benediction, houses built of prayer; the matter of faith in temples, a gate to high experience: behold, I testify in the Mystical Holy of Holies, the sanctuary of speaking sym-

133

bols and the Rosy Cross. ✠ According to the golden legend and the discovery of its inwritten parable, the maxims of a spiritual mystery were graven about the altar, in the vault of a hidden shrine. NEQUAQUAM VACUUM. There is no void of distance between the dedicated soul and God. Consecrate your hearts in dedication, and God shall be found within. LEGIS JUGUM: The bondage of the old law becomes the yoke of Christ. LIBERTAS EVANGELII: The liberty of the Gospel is the freedom of the soul in union with the Great Task-Master Who ordains the law of love. DEI GLORIA INTACTA: To the glory of God inviolate, world without end in love. ✠ Conversion of all conversions, change of change, stars out of dust arising, making of all things new: Be ye transmuted therefore from dead stones into living philosophical stones, shining on everlasting hills, radiant on the mount of God.

The pause of a moment follows: it is greatly still and expectant. A voice of victory proclaims:

THE HIGH PRIEST *(vel alius):* ORDO SANCTISSIMUS ROSEAE ET AUREAE CRUCIS.

The Rose Cross suspended in the black darkness gives forth its light suddenly. It appears in mid-air, and there is a passing of veiled figures beneath it, amidst smoke of thuribles.

THE HIGH PRIEST: Behold the cross of glory, the Rosy Cross, the sign without of God Who dwells within. The mighty cosmos of created things is made without: make Thou our world within. We have built all temples in Thy Holy Name:

134

build Thou the church within us. Abide and bless by Thine indwelling Presence.

At a battery of one knock the Holy Congregation rises, with the Celebrants and Spokesmen of the Rite, wherever they are placed in the temple.

THE HIGH PRIEST: The Tree of the Rosy Cross is Christ; the Tree is Life; the Tree is the Word made flesh: Immanuel, God is with us. It is also the manifest state of our humanity; and then the Rose signifies the Immanent Divinity, Which dwells within us, at once hidden and revealed. I bear my witness further that the Rose is the soul in man; and then the glittering point of dew, as the jewel within the centre, is the inward and hidden Christhood.

At a battery of one knock, the seats are resumed by all. The Rose-Cross continues to radiate in the darkness and again the music breathes. A voice of song tells of the Mystic Rose.

THE PRIESTESS OF THE RITE *(vel alia):* ROSA AUREA, ROSA SANCTA, ROSA VICTORIAE, ROSA MYSTICA, ROSA IMMORTALIS, ROSA COELI, ROSA FOEDERIS, ROSA SANCTISSIMA, ROSA DEITATIS, ROSA SALUTARIS NOSTRAE, ROSA UNITATIS, O PURISSIMA, O SANCTISSIMA, DULCIS ROSA CHRISTI.

The music continues for a space after the voice is hushed. The clouds of incense rise.

THE PRIESTESS OF THE RITE: The Rose art Thou, and we are the Rose in Thee: we are also a chaplet of roses about Thy morning star. The flower of the field is mine and this is the Holy Rose: I have bound Thy lilies on my heart. My rose expands in Thy light. The dew of Thy Presence falls therein, and it breathes forth fragrance of the Spirit. O ROSA FLORESCENS.

THE HIGH PRIEST: The Holy of Holies within this holy temple is also the Holy Rose. Let us be mindful of this jewel in the center and contemplate the Presence in the sanctuary, in the blessed place of the Presence.

There is again complete darkness, for the light of the Rosy Cross is withdrawn after these words, and there follows a great silence. The temple is a house of souls, and by those who think in the heart it shall be found a house of knowledge.

At the end of this contemplation:

THE HIGH PRIEST: By whom were you made a brother ?

HERALD OF THE RITE *(in the west):* By God and a good friend: so help me God.

SPOKESMAN OF THE RITE *(unus vel alter):* May joy and benediction, the power and mercy of God be with us this day and forever in the place of Divine mystery.

SECOND SPOKESMAN: Into Thy hands, O Lord: in the mercy of Thy hands abide the souls of the chosen ones.

THIRD SPOKESMAN: Sacred is he who maintains in his heart sacredly this high and sacred doctrine.

SPOKESMAN OF THE RITE: Be with us henceforth, O Master, through all our ways of quest, as Thou art and were from the beginning even unto the perfect end, the endless end of being.

SECOND SPOKESMAN: Visit us in the redemption of Thy knowledge.

THIRD SPOKESMAN: Change Thou our death in separation to the Life which is Life in Thee.

THE PRIESTESS OF THE RITE: May the Spirit of Thy Light enlighten, Thy Spirit of Wisdom strengthen, the Spirit of Understanding rule in heart and mind. O Inward Spirit, Guide and Ward in all: VENI, CREATOR SPIRITUS.

UNA ANCILLA TEMPLI: Thy Spirit is in those who love Thee: give unto us Thine Holy Spirit.

ANCILLA ALIA: Crown the humble with wisdom: marry us into perfect union.

THE HIGH PRIEST: For us who are Thine only set open doors of entrance to Thine Eternal Presence, the secret abode of Thy Glory.

THE PRIESTESS OF THE RITE: I testify concerning the way of the soul in love and the term attained therein. The reign of law is love, which rules in all. There is one law alone, one rule and reign, and love is love for ever. Love is the key and love the keeper of keys, the treasure within and the only lock that opens. The key of love is also the key of tongues, the living word within and the word expressed. The kingdom sought without and found within, the throne erected there, the scepter and the crown are Thine and Thou, O Love, Kinghood and King in all. I preach this gospel in all my parts of being.

ANCILLA UNA TEMPLI: The path of the life to come is a path of love.

ANCILLA ALIA: The love which dies for love is love that lives.

ANCILLA UNA: The love which lives through death is love immortal.

ANCILLA ALIA: Give me everlasting titles, the love that kills.

THE PRIESTESS OF THE RITE: O school of wisdom, school of perfect love: thereafter nothing dies, for death is dead.

There is music of the dead for a brief space, and then a voice cries in the darkness:

SPOKESMAN OF THE RITE: The perfect peace is with thee: thou art the peace of God, O blessed mystic death !

SECOND SPOKESMAN: Thy veils dissolved reveal the life beyond.

THIRD SPOKESMAN: Thine other names are vision, life in God, and after this the union.

THE HIGH PRIEST: The second birth of souls is a birth in love. I testify concerning the beginning of all mysteries and that which qualifies for all, the second birth of souls. Let us contemplate the mystery of love, and this abides within us.

The silence which follows is like the threshold of a world of experience behind the world of symbols, and at the end this contemplation dissolves in an organ reverie, a suggestion of deep things heard from the beginning in the heart, when the heart is still. The next theme is of the Hidden Master and the old foundation of the Rosy Cross.

THE HIGH PRIEST: The sacraments are not the life, but its sacred signs and veils. The signs are silent only when the soul is deaf. The wonder is not in their speaking but because so few can hear. ✠ There is fruit of life in symbols, for those who can penetrate green thickets and enter the orchard be-

139

hind. Till then we dwell in the precincts: we feed upon outward shells of images, and we drink their wine. O deeper hunger and that other thirst! ✠ Give me the real presence in place of all the pictures and pallid portraits only drawn in thought. What shall give life to the pictures, mind and speech in all? Thought of the soul, thought in the deep soul, and God uplifting soul in thought within. ✠ I have crossed the threshold: I have parted embroidered curtains: I have questioned oracles in speaking darkness, in the pregnant solitudes, in lone untrodden regions of the soul. ✠ I have opened a secret wall in my own house and have found a vault beyond. The Hidden Master of the Rosy Cross spoke to my secret soul. ✠ A light in the dark uplifted: I found a lamp therein, and it goes not out for ever. ✠ I knew him of whom I had read in the old days, when the spirit of quest was on me, in the old traditional tale of our Loving Father. He came unto me then in the youth of thought, as a son of the Spirit and bride born in the body of man, as Christ was born in a stable. He led the inner life in a house of religion, a house of contemplation, even a house of thought. ✠ There is an orient of the soul, and this may visit from on high: it is said that he travelled eastward. Was it not the Far East, the font and source and spring? There is no other travelling which counts as such for those who look to find the ends of being. ✠ We are told that he came unto his own and that his own received him, in the Hidden City. Was it not built upon the Mountain, a high uplifted place of holy mind? When we strip off the crude vestures, which are those of outward myth, it is found that he who came from the Center returned there and drew therefrom. ✠ He was given back to the world in the power of mission. He brought with him from the Center that experience which is high doctrine and an art of life in God. He came in the power of teaching, as if again unto his own in the bond of outward things, and they heard him not. But a few heard him within, and he built up his Brotherhood of the Rosy Cross, as if a church invisible and a house of the Holy Spirit. ✠ I say unto you, brethren, that there is the story of Christ on earth, in Palestine and its Holy Fields, and there is the Mystical Christ within: two stories, one at the root in the Theosophia of the Rosy Cross. And that of our Loving Father is also yours and mine: the vault of His house is within us, and the Center is also there. ✠ I have made unto myself a sepulcher: Lord Christ, arise therein. The Rosicrucian doctrine was: In Nobis Regnat Jesus, and it is understood thus among us. The connotation is Deus Nobiscum; Pax Profundia; Immanuel: God is with us. In one and the same sense, I testify therefore on the faith of the old claim, which has been with us from the beginning, that the Fellowship of the Rosy Cross is with the Father and Jesus. The synonym of all is Ecce Regnum Dei Intus. Peace profound, my Brethren, the stillness and its deep.

The Rosy Cross is manifested again in its light of splendor, and at a battery of one knock, the Holy Congregation rises and remains standing, while the deep sacramental meaning is shown forth as follows:

A Spokesman of the Rite: Mysterium Roseae et Aurem Crucis: Christ in manifestation, hidden and cosmic Christ.

SECOND SPOKESMAN: MEA VICTORIA IN CRUCE ROSEA: My victory is in the Rosy Cross. Immortal life removes the sting of death: Thou art our Life, O Lord.

THIRD SPOKESMAN: CRUX CHRISTI CORONA CHRISTIANO-RUM: Crown us in the part of our manifestation with the fruits of the work within.

THE PRIESTESS OF THE RITE: The soul is a rose awaiting consecration by the Spirit.

UNA ANCILLA TEMPLI: The rose of our desire becomes the Holy Rose.

ANCILLA ALIA: Rose of Jericho, Rose of Salem, Rose of the world below, Rose of the Paradise above: hide us in Thy sacred petals.

The light of the Rosy Cross is withdrawn after these words, and at a battery of one knock, their seats are resumed by all.

THE PRIESTESS OF THE RITE *(vel alia):* The unknown country of our inward being becomes the Kingdom of God when the Guide—who is Love within— brings us to the holy place and opens the door thereof, which leads to the Holy of Holies and the Presence therein. The Guide is that which is said in an old traditional story to lead the seeker of the Rosy Cross up a mountain in the midst of the earth, otherwise at the middle place of the world.

I say unto you that this Mountain is within and that it

is found at our own center. It is a place of many treasures which the world does not value, because they do not bear its marks or come out of its mints, as current coin accepted in its houses of exchange. It is said to be encompassed by cruel beasts and ravening birds, which are the evil passions within us — all the false desires. They are the lawless part of our nature in all the ways of life, the spirit of the world within us which strives with the Spirit of God. But on the brink, as it may be, of formless swamps of being, in death and the shadow of death, we have remembered the promise of life — of life for evermore and ever more of life.

We have heard the voice of the Guide, a music which wakens the secret deeps of soul and thence evokes response. He has come at our bidding, has opened a door of the heart and entered to abide within. We have contemplated in the heart because of him and have followed the lead of love, the lead that is Thine, O Lord, for love is Thine and Thou. When the desire of it has possessed us utterly, when the night is very dark within, then in a great silence the quest begins for the mountain. It is reached at midnight, the middle night of the soul, when all the passions are stilled, all images of sense obscured. But that which devolves upon the seeker is to call from his heart on God, a voice upraised in very deep of soul: for now the end is nigh.

The lion and the dragon, the eager birds of prey shall fly before that which is our Guard, as well as Guide in Paths. I say to you: Believe and find. In a wind of the Spirit you shall go up the hidden mountain. All that is of dead stone in your nature shall be rent like rocks; all that is perishable shall be consumed like earthly dross: there shall follow a great calm.

The dawn and the day-star shall rise on the mount of God, and the place of the treasure shall unveil. In the images of the old parable that treasure is a highest tincture, which might turn the world to gold. But this is the gold of God, according to another witness of the Rosy Cross, and this transmutes the soul. O Fount of life and health, Spirit and Presence of God: hereof is the Presence within, according to the picture-language, and such the hidden treasure of the secret mountain.

The place of the treasure in another mode of symbolism is a temple on the mountain-top, which is earth of the world to come and the land of the living. What laws of God come forth from this summit of Horeb to those who cross, with love their guide, the arid wastes of Sinai? And what transfiguration takes place on this mystic Tabor? The Rosy Cross bears witness to the high tincture, the Eternal Life thereof. That which is called the mountain in this old speaking allegory is known by other names in other types of legend. It is the spiritual citadel which contains the true stone and talisman of philosophers, a gift which remains to eternity, though all things else dissolve. It is called the glory of the world and way of truth, the hidden sacrament of the Rosy Cross and the only path to life. It is also the true elixir. But however we multiply images, and there is a cloud of others in the radiant lore of old, in reality it is one thing only — a state of inward being attained in love. It is reached by contemplation, when the soul eludes the methodical processes of the past and buries itself in love. It enters then into the great reality of being — which is its own reality — and finds its object in the height of ungenerated self; for there and thus only is God within.

The Herald of the Rite unveils his lantern and then rising, elevates it in the middle west.
HERALD: The deeps explore the height, but height and deep are one in love. The mind of earth unto the sanctuary of hidden mind lifts up its pallid light.

The sanctuary is made dimly visible and the high altar. The Celebrants and Ministers are shadowed vaguely forth.

HERALD: From the court of the temple to the Holy Place, Master, command Thy servants. Open the gate which leads to the Holy of Holies. Thou have given to us service in quest: call us to serve in attainment at Thine inmost shrine.

The lantern is veiled and the Herald resumes his scat.

UNA ANCILLA TEMPLI: The records of experience, the doctrines based thereon, the great antique systems, the immemorial faiths have taught us from the beginning that God is without; but in the mystery of love and this only is the authentic finding of God — far and how far from the common wear and tear of devotional use and wont.

ANCILLA ALIA: HABITAVIT IN NOBIS. He has dwelt in us from the beginning, but it is not as in a local habitation: it is as the self alone within.

ANCILLA UNA: We hear of Him only without, and the records are a portrait everywhere of an absent person.

ANCILLA ALIA: We set up images in all our temples, and they are reproduced as images in the mind: not these is He.
ANCILLA UNA: And the stories of the Great Masters are those of inward realizations that are theirs and not ours.

ANCILLA ALIA: O blessed lights upon the way, Christ-stories under many titles: the task is to make them ours, as all in truth are His, shadows or bright reflections of the one great work of souls, and He the head of the work.

THE PRIESTESS OF THE RITE: The one irrepealable condition is a selfless state without, for this alone makes free the secret path to reach the self within.

THE HIGH PRIEST: The secret mountain is the higher mind, MONS RATIONABILIS indeed, as it is called in the old chronicle concerning SUMMUM BONUM. That which is above encompasses that which is below and yet remains above, fulfilling and not destroying. It is the mind which sees by comprehension, the all-containing mind, an uplifted mode and state, as the logical understanding is another and lower mode.

A SPOKESMAN OF THE RITE: Raise us into eternal life, O Master, the state of the fixed stone, which is gold in the soul of man.

SECOND SPOKESMAN: O hard and stubborn flints, ground in the mills of God, for the separation of gold within and hidden gems of price, the chrysolyth and jasper of the eternal foundation.

THIRD SPOKESMAN: The Divine Presence is hidden in our natural manhood and revealed when this is transmuted by the work of Divine alchemy.

SPOKESMAN OF THE RITE: The transmutation is from within in spiritual alchemy, unlike the work in the crucible, as dreamed of old.

SECOND SPOKESMAN: The mystic stone is within us and transmutes all things. The authentic affirmation is therefore: Behold, I make all things new.

THIRD SPOKESMAN: But it is the soul above all things which becomes Spiritual Gold.

THE HIGH PRIEST: These are the stages of the process in the old parabolic terms: (1) Mortification, for that which can die must die: being perishable, it is not ours; (2) the Black State, which is one of figurative death completed, and these two correspond in official theology to the work of an instrument which is termed sufficing grace: for us it is a grade of love; (3) the White State, begotten by plenary grace, or Divine Love raised to its second degree; (4) The Red State, attained in the operation of super-essential grace, otherwise the third grade which is that of transcending love, possessing and possessed by God. In the Black State the evil body of desire is dead as such; the White State is manifestation of the soul in its purity; but the Red State is that of the Spirit in its splendor, and this is the Christ-Spirit. It is the state of espousals and union, of being redeemed by the blood of Christ, for the blood is the life. Herein is the great mystery of the sanctuary, which is the Second Advent, the return of the Personal Christ.

The Priestess of the Rite: Tinge Thou our hearts and make us gold for Thee, that we in turn may tincture.

The High Priest: Tinctura Christus Est: our medicine Thou.

Spokesman of the Rite: A saving fire within, a fire of healing. I testify on the part of the Masters that there is a golden tincture which is called the center of nature.

Second Spokesman: The fire of Divine Love is the eternal tincture of souls.

Third Spokesman: O blessed ineffable state, which the Masters called philosophical from the first days of our mystery.

The Priestess of the Rite: The stone that the builders rejected and all the wise of this world is set at the head of the corner in the eternal foundation, the keystone of a sacred arch which sustains the worlds.

Una Ancilla Templi: The first stone, proved and precious, the stone laid in Zion, a living stone, hewn without hands from the everlasting hill and hidden mount of God.

Ancilla Alia: The Lord is my rock and my stone: Thou, O Lord, my Savior.

The High Priest: Petra Autem Christus: way and truth and life.

The High Priest rises in his place. The Herald of the Rite gives a battery of one knock and all present stand up. The light above the throne is kindled suddenly and the High Priest is seen clearly, elevating a cubic stone which has reposed beside him on a pedestal. A voice in the sanctuary cries: Petra Fundebat Mihi Rivos Olei. The light is extinguished, the High Priest resumes his throne, the Herald repeats his battery and all present are seated.

There follows hereon the pause of a few moments, as the peace of Christ Indwelling.

The Priestess of the Rite: In Silentio et Spe: Silence of the indrawn soul and hope of light therein.

Una Ancilla Templi: Omnia Ab Uno et Omnia ad Unum: From God thou art and to God shalt thou return.

Ancilla Alia: Unum Sunt Omnia, Per Quod Omnia: the secret doctrine rings its golden changes.

THE HIGH PRIEST: DEUS VENDIT SUA DONA PRO LABORE: The Kingdom of Heaven suffers violence, and this is the sense thereof. The wages of God are eternal life.

A clear bell sounds within the sanctuary: The Rose-Cross gives forth its light suddenly. The Herald of the Rite stands up and speaks from the far west.

HERALD: EGREDERE PER VIAM CRUCIS: INGREDERE PER VITAM LUCIS: our comings forth and goings in are Thine.

He resumes his seat.

PRIESTESS OF THE RITE: Rose of Jericho, spiritual rose, rose of Heaven above, redeeming rose below. FLOREBIT REGNUM DEI INTUS QUASI ROSA ET LILIUM. The lilies bloom in the valley, even the Valley of Jehoshaphat.

THE HIGH PRIEST: We raise the plant within, the mystic rose: make it a rose without. From hidden ways of inward being, so the Christ comes forth; so lifted on the cross of life He bears the cosmic witness of Divinity to the Divine in man; so all His own draws after Him; and on the inward side and outward, sealing, they are sealed with God.

And now the lights go up: there is splendor of light everywhere. All present are standing up, alike in the Holy sanctuary and in the body-general of the temple. The banners are lifted up: the sacred incense fumes.

HERALD *(from his place):* Thy day, O Lord: to the dawn of the coining day and the joy of life therein.

THE HIGH PRIEST: The star of morning rises: the work of Light begins. The heart of man is the place of the morning star: Shine, O star of life, even to the perfect day.

THE PRIESTESS OF THE RITE: Shine also, Rosy Cross, the type without of all the grace within. I testify that this holy temple is the sanctuary of God, a spiritual palace, a sacred place, reserved to a holy priesthood.

THE HIGH PRIEST: The Order is Elias Artista, prophet and faithful witness of the hidden church.

THE PRIESTESS OF THE RITE: It testifies here and now to the coming of the blessed kingdom: all the great things are nigh.

THE HIGH PRIEST: MAGNALIA DEI ET NATURAE: Grace of the Lord within, glory and grace of heart: Splendor of the outward Presence; all nature shines in royal light of God.

THE PRIESTESS OF THE RITE: MYSTERIARCHA DEI: the signs without, the portents seen within are Thine, O Master. The omens of two worlds bespeak Thy Presence and bring Thy gospel tidings.

THE HIGH PRIEST: An eye of the soul looks in towards things eternal and an eye looks out on time.

THE PRIESTESS OF THE RITE: The mortal eye is overwhelmed with glory; but the soul abides therein which is turned to Thee.

THE HIGH PRIEST: It was said of old in the records of the Rosy Cross that within us and not without is that which we seek in our folly without instead of within.

THE PRIESTESS OF THE RITE: Make unto us a still Sabbath, and within us the Word shall speak.

THE HIGH PRIEST: That which is without comes forth from the first matter and returns thereto: that which is within goes back to God, Who is its source. For ever and evermore, it is God and the soul only, the soul alone and God, a perpetual intercourse, an unity in the ground and root. It is therefore OMNIA SUNT RES UNA on the external plane, but EST UNA SOLA RES on the side of inward reality.

Having put away their respective wands in their rests, the High Priest and the Priestess leave their thrones and meet at a middle point of the sanctuary, some distance behind the altar. They stand side by side with faces towards the west. The cubic stone is in the hands of the High Priest.

THE HIGH PRIEST: All things are one only.

THE PRIESTESS OF THE RITE: On earth as is in Heaven.

THE HIGH PRIEST: Proceeding on earth from one substance of the wise.

THE PRIESTESS OF THE RITE: And in Heaven from one God Almighty and Father of all.

THE HIGH PRIEST: In Christ revealed within.

THE PRIESTESS OF THE RITE: The higher soul.

THE HIGH PRIEST: Christ and the Christ-State.

THE PRIESTESS OF THE RITE: Amen. O inexpressible deep of Deity.

They pass by south to the altar, preceded respectively by the great banner of the Rosy Cross and that of the Heavenly Rose. The Thurificantes at the horns of the altar hand them their thuribles. They proceed in succession to the altar, the banner bearers facing east, at a little distance behind them. The High Priest deposits the great cubic stone in its place between the small cubes. He puts incense about the Altar, CUM SIGNO ✠ CRUCIS. (In the sign of the cross.)

THE HIGH PRIEST: Thou Who art first and only, from and beyond the aeons: to Thee in adoration of the soul, till all the soul is Thine.

He turns, censing towards the west ✠ and over the Holy Congregation.

THE HIGH PRIEST: The powers of the soul are an incense offered by the inward man as a sacrifice to his Creator.

He goes back by the north to his throne, preceded by the great banner. The Priestess of the Rite puts incense about the altar, CUM SIGNO ✠ CRUCIS.

THE PRIESTESS OF THE RITE: AD MAJOREM ROSEM ✠ Crucis Gloriam.

She turns, censing towards the west ✠ *and over the Holy Congregation.*

THE PRIESTESS OF THE RITE: The dew in the center of the rose is ROS FRUCTIFICANS, the spirit which is life of soul. SOLI DEO HONOS ET GLORIA.

The Priestess goes back by the north to her throne, preceded by the banner of the Heavenly Rose. All resume their seats, within and without the sanctuary.

THE HIGH PRIEST: The stability and equipoise of the universe are the good pleasure of the Lord made manifest.

THE PRIESTESS OF THE RITE: The seals of the Divine covenant are imprinted on the whole body of nature.

THE HIGH PRIEST: Divinity is archetypal and nature reflects Divinity, so that it is one of God'S great witnesses to the world of the soul within.

154

THE PRIESTESS OF THE RITE: In this way the soul is everywhere encompassed by the natural and supernatural means of its inward return to God.

THE HIGH PRIEST: All the reflected lights lead us to the True Light.

THE PRIESTESS OF THE RITE: The whole order of the cosmos moves with him who has taken his heart in his hands and has said: I will go up to the altar of God.

THE HIGH PRIEST: Let us therefore remember holiness, that we may stand in the Presence of the King, Who reigns over the world within as well as the world without.

THE PRIESTESS OF THE RITE: Remember also the everlasting kinship of the heart with that which it desires in the height.

THE HIGH PRIEST: Awaiting the high light of all, let us be faithful in the small things, that we may be worthy of our faith in the great.

THE PRIESTESS OF THE RITE: God answers all souls that call upon Him and is invoking continually from within, that the soul may be turned and answer.

THE HIGH PRIEST: The way of the SUMMUM BONUM is by the sacrifice of that which matters nothing to attain that which is All.

THE PRIESTESS OF THE RITE: An All in all of height and deep within, and God in all forever.

THE HIGH PRIEST: We have left the carved Gods and dead idols of the Gentiles, having heard of that one thing which abides in the life of the center.

THE PRIESTESS OF THE RITE: We have been satisfied too long with a part, who were meant for the whole.

THE HIGH PRIEST: The part is separation, the whole is union: our will is to the whole in Thee.

The Herald of the Rite gives a battery of one knock and rises up.

HERALD: The first steps taken in the Path of Union are taken by the will of man. ✠There is one within the threshold who brings the will to serve, the will to walk among us, looking in these sacred precincts for a way of life in God.

THE HIGH PRIEST: The pearl of great price is hidden, and the path or way of its discovery demands the whole man.

HERALD: He has dwelt in the cities of this world; he has fared through the waste places: he seeks to abide in God.

THE HIGH PRIEST: Pilgrim of outward life, what of the life within?

THE POSTULANT *(who is prompted):* I seek its ways through all my clouds of darkness.

THE HIGH PRIEST: What dwells within?

THE POSTULANT *(who is prompted):* The Kingdom of Heaven is there, for the finding of those who know.

THE HIGH PRIEST: Who rules and reigns therein?

THE POSTULANT *(who is prompted):* Christ Mystical, the inward Christ and higher soul of man. I make an act of faith and look in God to see.

THE PRIESTESS OF THE RITE: World without end. Amen.

She has risen with the Ancillae Templi and thereafter resumes her seat, also with them.

THE HIGH PRIEST: The Order's Godspeed in its work to the Glory of God is pronounced upon this serving brother.

THE PRIESTESS OF THE RITE: On the faith of perpetual silence, according to the covenant with God, may God be with thee forever in the bonds of our holy society.

She returns to her throne, escorted by the banner-bearers, who also resume their places. The High Priest proceeds by south round the altar, and the Ushers, separating their palms, go back to the west. The Postulant remains on his knees, and the High Priest draws to his side at the altar. All others are seated. The sealed Rituale is taken by the High Priest from the hands of the Postulant and is elevated towards the east.

THE HIGH PRIEST: We lift up our books without: be Thou our Book within.

It is now placed on the altar, and the hands of the High Priest are extended above the Postulant.

THE HIGH PRIEST: DEUS NOBISCUM: PAX PROFUNDA. The great purpose is within and the Divine event: Seek therefore without no longer for that which is within. Remember also that we have to lose what the world prizes before we can attain the All. You carry much baggage, my brother; but henceforth you shall go lighter, if yours is the will to freedom.

He takes the wallet of the Postulant and turning westward upholds it in the sight of the beloved congregation.

THE HIGH PRIEST: FRATRES ET SORORES, we know in the world without, according to the wisdom of its prince, that ever they prefer the robber, and so is the robber released to them and the Christ is crucified.

He takes out and exposes the inscribed contents successively and then casts them on the ground.

THE HIGH PRIEST: The lust of the flesh; the lust of the eyes; and the pride of life: ADORO TE DEVOTE, LATENS LUCIFER.

He lifts up the empty wallet.

THE HIGH PRIEST: They made of it a den of thieves; but in the sacramental power and grace of my high office, I have cast out the money-changers from this natural temple of humanity, that henceforth it may be a house of prayer, for such is the house of God.

He turns again to the Postulant.

THE HIGH PRIEST: I give unto you unblemished tokens of the life to come within you. Say therefore, now and henceforward: ADORO TE DEVOTE, LATENS DEITAS.

This is repeated by the Postulant, and the white of white cubes on the altar are placed in the pilgrim's wallet.

THE HIGH PRIEST: I pray that your natural manhood may so be changed in God.

The wallet is hung on the left wrist of the Postulant, who is raised, from his knees, and it is said in so doing:

THE HIGH PRIEST: Be thou a branch of that Tree which God planted in Paradise.

This is followed immediately by a voice raised in the sanctuary.

A SPOKESMAN OF THE RITE: It is written: Every tree which bringeth not forth good fruit shall be cut down and cast into the fire.

But the allusion in this case is to an observance practiced by the Order under certain circumstances, and the maxim concerning it is therefore: ABSIT OMEN. The Postulant is faced to the High Priest, mid-wise at the altar.

THE HIGH PRIEST: By gifts from Heaven and not by arts of earth or earthly mind be Heaven conceived and known; and in thy soul be earth as Heaven revealed. By faithful service at the sacred gate, the soul is taught and finds perchance therein how other gates may open.

Thereafter, and both being turned to the west:

THE HIGH PRIEST: FRATRES ET SORORES, in the liberty and election of our sacred mystery, I give unto you a serving brother of the Rosy Cross. He that is faithful and true shall receive a new name among us. Meanwhile he is FRATER UN-DECIMUS *(vel numerus alius)* and is enrolled as such among the Keepers of the Sacred Precincts.

The Ushers of the Rite come up by the north, and the Postulant is led to his former seat in the west. The bearer of the great banner proceeds by south to the altar and goes before the High Priest, who returns to his throne in the sanctuary, all standing up therein to receive him in due form, and all resuming their seats as he takes his own. There is the pause of a brief period, and it is like the heart in its stillness, when the heart is hushed in God. It may close again in organ music, and the First Spokesman of the Rite rises with arms lifted up and says in reverential clearness:

SPOKESMAN OF THE RITE: The beginning and the end are God. Amen.

The sealing word of the rite is repeated by all in the sanctuary, and he resumes his seat. The Herald of the Rite rises with a battery of one knock.

HERALD OF THE RITE: To the end therefore in love, and this is the Higher Soul. FRATRES ET SORORES IN ORDINE ROSEAE CRUCIS, I say unto you that this soul is Christ.

THE PRIESTESS OF THE RITE: The means of livelihood are means of love in this our life of the mysteries.

THE HIGH PRIEST: Who quotes in any houses of exchange the everlasting values? Who deals therein? Who buys or sells?

HERALD: The everlasting values are treasured in the heart of man, when God has changed the heart. I open my accounts therein: I sell and buy forever.

He resumes his seat.

THE HIGH PRIEST: I certify that the self-knowing part, illuminated by the good, the beautiful and the true — VERITAS, VITA, VIA — is in the state of abiding love.

THE PRIESTESS OF THE RITE: A world withdrawn beyond the world of vision.

THE HIGH PRIEST: At the back of the centuries the voice of the Rosy Cross bears witness that such an unity in spirit with Christ is possible here and now.

THE PRIESTESS OF THE RITE: Not from without descending and not a soul infused, or master part to servant part attesting, I bear my faithful witness that Christ Mystical, the inward Christ, is a state, a spirit in attainment.

THE HIGH PRIEST: And these mysteries are hidden, for the titles of their knowledge are within.

THE PRIESTESS OF THE RITE: That which is within is older than that which is without, and it has come from far away.

THE HIGH PRIEST: While abiding in things without, the great practical secret is to keep ourselves sacredly.

THE PRIESTESS OF THE RITE: Dedicated, pure and naked, turn we the soul within.

THE HIGH PRIEST: Let us make the world without as the world within and things material even as things of the spirit.

THE PRIESTESS OF THE RITE: If the center of the soul is God; let it be so within us that this Center is everywhere and the circumference nowhere.

THE HIGH PRIEST: The outward quests become the quest of souls when doors like these are opened: till then indeed we know not what we do.

THE PRIESTESS OF THE RITE: We wait for the time of the quickened soul, the open heart and eye.

THE HIGH PRIEST: The time of a Birth in God, a Second Birth of souls.

There is the pause of a few moments, as when a soul is stilled in contemplation. A voice rises suddenly over its well of silence. It may be that of the Priestess, of one of the Ancillae Templi or a Spokesman of the Rite. There is no ruling hereon, and it may be accompanied or not by organ music. It intones or chants

THE SACRED INVOCATION

✠

I. Souls of the Holy Ones, souls of the Second Birth, abide and bless.

II. Souls of the Christhood, souls at the term of quest, abide and bless.

III. Spirit of the cosmic world, spirit of the Lord therein, abide and bless.

IV. Thou Who art present in all, Thou Who transcendest all, abide and bless.

✠

The silence that follows is again only of moments, as of one who says in his heart: IMPLORA PACEM. Thereafter the colloquy continues and assumes a deeper note.

THE HIGH PRIEST: Concentered purpose culminates, a vibrant point of life.

THE PRIESTESS OF THE RITE: The end is repose of consciousness in infinite love and of infinite love in consciousness.

THE HIGH PRIEST: There is no God but God, and He is found within.

THE PRIESTESS OF THE RITE: Herein is the first and last, in comparison with which there is no second, and none whereby we can enter — after all the warfare — into peace.

THE HIGH PRIEST: We look towards that time when the glory of the Lord shall transfigure the man without and the robe of our priesthood become the robe of glory, of which it is the type and figure in our world of emblems.

THE PRIESTESS OF THE RITE: There is neither outward nor inward: I am Thine within and without; and in this unity — world without end for ever — there is Thou, O Lord, alone.

THE HIGH PRIEST: DATUM IN MONTE ABIEGNO.

He gives the battery of the grade - one knock - and all rise, within and without the sanctuary.

THE HIGH PRIEST: The paradise below is the state of attainment as it is possible here and now: in our time-immemorial symbols, it is said to be manifest and hidden in a secret place of the earth. It is a holy school of the spirit, and its witness is the Rosy Cross.

THE PRIESTESS OF THE RITE: Make pure the mind; dissolve the heart; renew the Soul.

THE HIGH PRIEST: But the paradise above is that which is super celestial and was said of old among us to be planted in the New Jerusalem. It is spirit of all things spiritual, and it is union in the eternal state.

THE PRIESTESS OF THE RITE: God in us, and we in God. Unto this last therefore, O Lord of All.

The silence which follows should be as a state out of space and time, in which no distinction exists. Thereafter the voice of the High Priest, who has moved to a middle point in the sanctuary, proclaims in high uplifted tones:

THE HIGH PRIEST: The Spirit returns to God Who gave it.

All present resume their seats, and the space of silence which follows shall be as the dream of a moment concerning an isle of rest. When this ends there is sung to its own music

THE HIGH HYMN OF THE PRESENCE

I. I have passed through the ways without in the light of these, amidst star-flowers, flowers of a bright star, the herb of silence and the herb of speech.

II. Voices of hills were round me, voices deep in vales; words which went over the cornfields; paths that found a voice;

rain of the waters of music, liquor of sound, liquescence of perfect melody.

III. The glory of all the glory, the joy of the life therein, splendor of solar days and starry nights were filled with rumors of Thee.

IV. I have seen the flight of stars and the quest of those who follow the quest of Thee, the work of Thy stars in their leading and planets in sacred vigils: I know of Thine inward strange upliftings on breaking through brush-wood and coming unawares to the sea.

V. A Spirit which is Thine in the river moves on through vale and hill; Thine is the strange communion of stream and sea, when the stream is received by the ocean: the lapping waves of lake and river lisp intelligible words.

VI. The dew is Thy wealth flowing over and a wine of fragrance; the rain is a choir full of anthems, and these are anthems of Thee: the leaves from their stalls make response in due order; and these responses are Thine.

VII. In language of fountains, light laughter of fountains, I hear of Thee: it is Thou and Thou only in golden showers of sunshine; in secrets of moonlight, Thou and only Thou.

VIII. The ways go further; the days move on: the rumor becomes a gospel, sounding above and below, over the land and sea, city and solitude.

IX. Wind-harps and echoes, echoes about the temple: in Sacred Fanes which man has built for God, I heard Thy Word of stillness behind the altar.

X. The words of power move about shrines and temples; the shrines vibrate; the white and gold of tabernacles breathe forth Thy presence.

XI. The silent measures between the beats of moments, words in the secret ear, pledges of sacred words: they bear Thy witness all the days of life.

XII. Do I not witness also and Thou from within me speak? Shall I not find Thee therefore, if only I seek within, behind the thought of the brain and love of the human heart?

XIII. It came about thus that while the whole world sang of Thee and Thy Presence, I heard an inward voice below, as it were, the voices, a music within the light.

XIV. A Spirit of Truth from unplumbed deeps within, it joined with the theme of that endless cosmic anthem, the news of Thee in another world of being.

XV. I have heard Thee and seen Thee in mine own shrine and temple, where the one true voice is Thine, the presence is only Thou, and all that belongs to self has died in the sacred precincts.

XVI. It is Thou for ever within: no part of all is mine, except in the surface sense of the things that pass. Praise unto the Great Reality: the Inward Self is Thou.

The Herald of the Rite gives a battery of one knock and all present rise. He goes before the Postulant, who is brought again to the altar.

THE HIGH PRIEST: The hidden house of the Holy One has neither bars nor locks. For those who wait upon the call, free ways are always open; and for those who are born in the sanctuary, the temple is with them ever in their daily ways. They do not come in or go out: they abide therein, its incense always round them and all its sacred chants. The candle of the Lord is with them, the hidden treasure and the Word of Life.

The High Priest proceeds by south to the altar. The Herald of the Rite takes the sealed RITUALE ROSEAE CRUCIS from the altar and presents it to him with bowed head, sAying:

HERALD: EVANGELIUM AETERNUM.

THE HIGH PRIEST *(in receiving it):* LIBER VITAE CHRISTUS.

He turns westward and exhibits it to the Holy Congregation.

THE HIGH PRIEST: The book of Life in the Rose.

The Postulant is turned about and directed to kneel before him. The High Priest lays the book upon his head.

THE HIGH PRIEST: To the manifestation without you, my brother, of the inward Christian Man.

He lifts up the book, arid the Herald raises the Postulant.

THE HIGH PRIEST: We have received you this day within the precincts of a temple which is dedicated to the quest of God. Behind it there is a door which opens on many paths leading to the greater mysteries, and within or behind these mysteries there is a central place of all, which is that of divine experience.

The Herald of the Rite places the Postulant in the south. He is so turned that he faces a great mirror immediately before him on the wall.

THE HIGH PRIEST: Contemplate in this glass of vision and behold the temple of our Sacred Rite prolonged into the far distance. What intervenes to hinder the free prospect? I say unto thee: It is thine own image in the foreground of the picture. Think well in the heart hereon. It tells of thy work to come, that which is put into thy hands and that none can do but thou, the effacement of thy lower personality in all its parts and modes: the desire of the flesh, the dedications of material mind and the will in separation from God. Be it ever remembered that their conquest is the victory of Divine Love. When thou hast prevailed in this holy war the mystic temple within thee shall reflect the personal self no longer, and in thine own Holy of Holies thou shalt behold the Presence.

The Postulant is faced to the west and the High Priest addresses the Holy Congregation.

THE HIGH PRIEST: The valediction of this sacred ceremony looks for a day to come when we shall meet at the Center.

The High Priest remains at the altar. The Ushers of the Rite come up by the north and take charge of the Postulant. A procession is formed in the sanctuary and passes by south to west. It is led by the Herald, whom the Ushers follow with the Postulant. It is brought up by the Priestess, who goes before the High Priest when he joins it at the proper point, the banner-bearers being in their due places.

The doors are opened by the Watcher, and the company passes out, followed by the congregation of the rite.

In the vestibule or other precinct of the temple, the High Priest hands to the Postulant a branch of palm, olive or other symbolical tree, to which a tablet is attached. Hereon he is required to write his full name, adding FRATER UNDECIMUS (vel numerus alius). When this has been done:

THE HIGH PRIEST: Beloved serving brother of the Rosy Cross and Keeper of its Sacred Precincts, this emblematical token of your reception among us will now be deposited in a cedar chest set apart for the preservation of similar evidential objects; and I trust that it will remain there until time immemorial. In the event of your resignation in good standing and for acceptable reasons, it will be reduced to ashes, for you will have ceased to be a branch of our mystical Tree of Life, and those ashes will be placed in their proper urn. But in case of your demission through neglect of the Order and its duties they will be returned to earth, that you who have forgotten the temple may be forgotten in turn by us. I wish you perfect peace among us and light from God therein, remembering the sacred covenants.

Those who are proved in this preliminary grade will find the veils of the Order lifted, that they may proceed further. Those who produce no warrants will remain as Watchers of the Holy House, whether or not they may witness other ceremonial observances as spectators only. If and when those who pass on enter into plenary possession of the rite, they will find that there is a sense in which they have received everything, as in far off summary or shadowed outline, in this ceremony of the threshold. On the other hand, if they go no further, in reality they will have received nothing, more especially if there is nothing in themselves by which they can be led onward.

✠ HERE ENDS THE RITUAL OF THE ROSY CROSS, APPOINTED FOR THE PRESENT DECENNIUM IN THE GRACE OF GOD AND TO HIS SERVICE. ✠

Milton Keynes UK
Ingram Content Group UK Ltd.
UKHW011300180724
15UKWH00020B/121/J